MW00632339

NEW YORK STATE ASSOCIATION OF INDEPENDENT SCHOOLS

INDEPENDENT
BY DESIGN

A History of the New York State Association of Independent Schools

INDEPENDENT
BY DESIGN

A History of the
New York State Association
of Independent Schools

DANE L. PETERS

Independent by Design: A History of the New York State Association of Independent Schools by Dane L. Peters

Published by The New York State Association of Independent Schools, 17 Elk Street (First Floor), Albany, NY 12207, (518) 694-5500. E-mail: info@nysais.org. Website: www.nysais.org

Printed in the United States of America.

Library of Congress Control Number: 2014947815

ISBN: 978-0-578-14542-6
Design, Typography, and Setup: Custom Communications, Inc., Saco, ME

Photo Credits: Front cover, title page, and back cover: iStock by Getty Images; Chapter 1 pp. 19, 26: courtesy of The Packer Collegiate Institute, Brooklyn, NY; Chapter 2 p. 61: courtesy of Lake Forest Country Day School, Lake Forest, IL; Chapter 3 p. 85: courtesy of The Harley School, Rochester, NY; p. 86: courtesy of Mohonk Mountain House, New Paltz, NY; Chapter 4 p. 113: courtesy of The Town School, New York, NY; Chapter 6 p. 151: courtesy of The Peck School, Morristown, NJ; p. 167: courtesy of Emma Willard School, Troy, NY; p. 169: courtesy of Robert Sheridan; p. 202: iStock by Getty Images. All other photos courtesy of The New York State Association of Independent Schools.

10 9 8 7 6 5 4 3 2 1

For families:
Chris's and my beautiful family
and
the NYSAIS family

Contents

FOREWORD

As is noted in the Introduction to this book, organizations, like people, go through distinctive stages in their development. In addition, organizations, like people, are shaped by the many events that surround them and, in turn, help shape and reshape those outside events. NYSAIS, at its core, is about independence and relationships. The immediate external event that propelled the creation of NYSAIS was an appellate court ruling acknowledging the importance of independent schools in the State of New York. This ruling caused our predecessors—Paul D. Shafer (Packer Collegiate Institute), Dorothy Brockway Osborne (Spence School), Anne Wellington (Emma Willard School), Philip M. B. Boocock (Nichols School), Charles W. Bradlee (Pebble Hill School), Howard I. Dillingham (Manlius School), Morton Snyder (Rye Country Day School), Frank Hackett (Riverdale Country School), Wilson Parkhill (Collegiate School), Harold C. Amos (Adelphi Academy), and Joseph Allen (Poly Prep Country Day School)—to attend a meeting in October 1947 from which the foundation for NYSAIS was formed. To this group we are deeply indebted.

When one of my predecessors, Steve Hinrichs, passed away in 2010, it became increasingly clear that those early NYSAIS voices were receding, limiting the opportunities to gather firsthand narratives about the founding and early years of our association. Fortunately, the NYSAIS Board of Trustees recognized the importance and timeliness of documenting our history and funded the current work in which we not only were able to gather information from the historical record, but were able to interview those who have continued to shape the fabric of the community that we call NYSAIS. To this group we are deeply indebted.

I am honored to be a part of the history of this vibrant educational community. We hope that future NYSAIS educators will enjoy reading about the people, programs, and events that formed their organization as they navigate the complex terrain, charting the course that will affect the hundreds of member schools and, more importantly, the tens of thousands of children who attend those schools.

Finally, this work would not be possible without the dedication of Dane Peters, former head of school at Brooklyn Heights Montessori School as well as a NYSAIS trustee. His love of history and writing, as well as of NYSAIS, is evident in the ways in which he has woven historical events, both internal and external, together into a compelling story. Those who follow us will, we hope, benefit from learning more about our rich history, because understanding our past helps us navigate our present while planning our future. To Dane we are deeply indebted.

Mark W. Lauria, Ph.D.
NYSAIS Executive Director

INTRODUCTION

The New York State Association of Independent Schools—most commonly referred to in the New York independent school community as NYSAIS (pronounced nie-saays)—is one of over 3,000 national, state, and regional educational associations in the United States. Of the thirty-plus state and regional associations devoted to independent schools, NYSAIS has the second-largest membership, with 194 schools—and growing—serving some 79,000 students in New York state.[1] (The reader will find these endnote reference numbers throughout the book; they correspond to numbers and related sources listed in the Notes section in the back of the book.)

NYSAIS is truly a family, in concept and operation. It has been nurturing, protecting, and championing its member schools since 1947, and what defines it as a family is the hard work and devotion of its staff and thousands of volunteers, all supporting a common mission. Without their support of each other, it would not—could not—be the leading association that it is today. *Independent by Design: A History of the New York State Association of Independent Schools* tells the story of the association from its birth to adulthood and beyond.

Nonprofit organizations go through stages of life, and there is one reference book that has been a beacon for associations, helping them understand these various phases. *Five Life Stages of Nonprofit Organizations* by Judith Sharken Simon delineates the stages as:

- Stage One: Imagine and Inspire. This beginning stage is where the organization is not yet formalized and where imagination and inspiration abound.

- Stage Two: Found and Frame. This is where the organization receives its official nonprofit status and all the activities of founding and framing the organization occur.
- Stage Three: Ground and Grow. Now the organization is concerned with building its foundation by grounding its activities and growing the "business."
- Stage Four: Produce and Sustain. The mature phase of the organization's life when production is at its peak and sustaining the organization is a high priority.
- Stage Five: Review and Renew. The organization is reinventing itself in some way, shape, or form through a process of review and renewal.[2]

Because NYSAIS is an educational nonprofit organization, it can also be helpful to frame its evolution using the child-development terms that educators use, as well as Sharken's model. Since the association's mission is to support the well-being of its member schools, and the fact that the member schools are all committed to caring for children—preschoolers through high school seniors—it only seems fitting to look at the evolution of NYSAIS using similar developmental stages. From birth through adulthood and beyond, we will look at the remarkable growth of an organization that began over 65 years ago.

So as to ensure that the voices are accurate and genuine throughout the association's infancy and elementary stages, those chapters are drawn directly from correspondence, minutes of the Board of Trustees and annual meetings, and Board of Trustees executive committee meetings. In subsequent stages—preadolescent and adolescent—the chapters are based on executive director reports and stories gathered through interviews. In the final chapter, adulthood, I use all of the previous resources and my own personal experiences with the association. I have watched NYSAIS grow from numerous vantage points: as Professional Development Committee chair, head of a member school, board member of the Guild of Independent Schools of New York, Accreditation Visiting Committee chair, a founder of the Assistant Heads Conference, director of the Beginning Teachers Institute, Experienced Teachers Institute faculty member, annual conference planner, chair of the Council on Professional Learning and Collaboration, member of all Think Tank sessions, presenter at conferences, member of the Executive Director Search Committee, secretary of the NYSAIS Board of Trustees, and now as part-time staff member.

Finally, in preserving the flavor of each decade, it is important to explore how the organization evolved and grew amid the tumult of state, national, and world events. Drawing upon the vast resources of the Internet, historical and cultural milestones—including wars, rock concerts, films, assassinations, bestselling books, technological innovations, and educational landmarks—are interspersed throughout to provide context for a growing organization in the greater world. It is within this context that the adult NYSAIS will live a long, productive life, supporting its mission, its member schools, and, most of all, its children. I am confident that it will continue to reinvent itself, thanks to the talents and tireless efforts of our members. It is an honor to be part of such a family.

CHAPTER ONE

Birth and Infant Years: 1940s and 1950s

In December 1941, just two years and two decades after the end of World War I, America found itself at war once more, when the Japanese bombing of Pearl Harbor finally drew the United States into World War II. Four years, over 400,000 American lives, and two atomic bombs later, World War II came to a close, and 12 million U.S. servicemen and women—also known as G.I.s—returned home to their families.[1] Little did anyone realize that this Greatest Generation would soon generate another kind of explosion: the Baby Boom, the postwar population explosion that would have such a dramatic impact on the American education system.

By 1948, just three years into the incubation of the baby boom generation, it was already clear that this new era would necessitate a new approach to education to accommodate this growing influx of children. The existing education model, inspired in part by the Industrial Revolution assembly line, was proving obsolete for this democratic country, and parents who demanded more for their children would increasingly look to private education for new alternatives. Be it parochial schools, boarding schools, or local day schools, people who had the means demanded a more personalized and less bureaucratic and politically engineered approach to their children's education.

New York's private school leaders were already reckoning with how to meet the challenges they faced, including regulation by the state. The impetus that inspired the president of Packer Collegiate Institute to form an independent school association was eloquently explained by NYSAIS's third executive director, Fred Calder, in his February–April 1998 *Bulletin*, "The Roots of Independence."

> Since 1925 the state and private schools have struggled to determine the line between reasonable and unreasonable regulations. In 1945 the State of New York drew a line. An act of the legislature required that all nonsectarian private elementary schools apply for registration and be subject to regulation by the commissioner of education. Packer Collegiate Institute refused to apply and, joined by sister schools, contested the law on constitutional grounds. Packer lost in the first instance and again lost unanimously at the appellate level. Finally, in 1948, Packer took the case to New York's highest tribunal, the Court of Appeals. On July 16, 1948, the Court struck down the Compulsory Registration Act by a 4-2 vote. But it was a close call. If one judge had voted the other way, the decision of the Appellate Division would have stood, and registration would have been the order of the day. Close though it may have been, much of our schools' freedom of action and independence has rested on the *Packer* case for the last half century.

Nevertheless, *Packer* was decided on narrow grounds. The Court did say that the legislature could not regulate private schools. To the contrary, it noted that, "The Legislature, under the police power, has a limited right to regulate such schools in the public interest." What the Court actually decided was that the legislature could not delegate broad, unspecified regulatory power to the commissioner of education, and thus the act was unconstitutional. When New York, mindful of *Packer*, introduced high school registration some years later, it was, theoretically, on a voluntary basis. But unless a school is registered, it cannot confer legal diplomas. So much for volunteerism. The nose of the camel enters the tent in devious ways.

So the point of this legal exposition is to say that the freedom of choice and action we enjoy as schools occupies a shifting space between government's limited but substantial power to regulate all precollegiate education and our constitutional right to exist and function independently. As various political forces sweep through the nation, the state tries repeatedly in the name of reform to bring the private schools to heel. Our schools, of course, have three choices. They may simply accede. They may negotiate. Or they may practice civil disobedience. In the real world what we actually do is to operate somewhere between negotiation and disobedience.[2]

This resolute independence from the state education establishment actually predated the genesis of NYSAIS, as is evident in a 1947 letter that Packer Collegiate's Paul D. Shafer sent to a circle of New York school heads.

April 17, 1947

Mr. Morton Snyder, Headmaster
Rye Country Day School
Rye, New York

My dear Mr. Snyder:

Some time ago the suggestion was made that some sort of State organization of independent schools be formed which could bring a united pressure to bear upon the legislature in Albany and the State Department of Education, on matters concerning the welfare of independent schools.

As you may know, the Packer Collegiate Institute is at the present time plaintiff in a suit against the State Department of Education to have declared unconstitutional the law requiring elementary schools, other than public and parochial, to register. Mr. Ingraham, our counsel, in preparing his case has found increasing evidence of the necessity for independent schools to be on the alert to protect themselves from both the unthinking persons who are concerned only with votes and those definitely unfriendly to private education. The experience of the schools, colleges, and universities of the State of New York in opposing the recent Austin-Mahoney Bill is an example of the need for careful scrutiny of bills, which are introduced and of united action in favoring or opposing them.

A number of schools heads throughout the State have talked about this matter from time to time. During the past week, Dr. Allen of Poly, Mr. Amos of Adelphi, and I chatted at some length about it. It was our belief, and one confirmed by other heads with whom we

NYSAIS founding president Paul D. Shafer, circa 1944.

It was our belief . . . that it would be a good plan to have a State organization of independent schools, the main purpose of which would be to protect such institutions from harmful legislation and directives.

—President Paul D. Shafer

had talked earlier, that it would be a good plan to have a State organization of independent schools, the main purpose of which would be to protect such institutions from harmful legislation and directives. We concluded that it would be well to have a small group of school heads from various areas in our State get together in the early fall to talk over a possible organization; if such a group would look favorably upon it, then a meeting of representatives of all of the independent schools of the State could be called for the purpose of setting up a formal organization. We should like very much to have you as a member of this founding group.

This letter is being addressed to the following:
Mrs. Harold S. Osborne, The Spence School, NYC, N.Y.
Miss Anne Wellington, Emma Willard School, Troy, N.Y.
Mr. Philip M. B. Boocock, Nichols School, Buffalo, N.Y.
Mr. Charles W. Bradlee, Pebble Hill School, DeWitt, N.Y.
Dr. Howard I. Dillingham, Manlius School, Manlius, N.Y.
Mr. Morton Snyder, Rye Country Day School, Rye, N.Y.
Dr. Frank Hackett, Riverdale Country School,
     Riverdale-on-Hudson, N.Y.
Mr. Wilson Parkhill, Collegiate School, NYC, N.Y.
Mr. Harold C. Amos, Adelphi Academy, Brooklyn, N.Y.
Dr. Joseph Allen, Poly Prep Country Day School,
     Brooklyn, N.Y.

We shall be very glad to have this group meet at the Packer Collegiate Institute some time in September or October, and I hope that you will be willing to take part in this preliminary discussion.

It is not the thought of any of us that another organization to hold meetings and conduct annual conventions is necessary. Our belief is that we need to be united in our efforts to protect private education in our State, and that is the only reason that we are suggesting that this organization be considered.

Sincerely yours,
President [Paul D. Shafer
Packer Collegiate Institute, Brooklyn]

The first official meeting of this new organization—consisting of the ten founders listed in the above letter, along with its author—took place on October 8, 1947 at the Albany Academy. It was at this meeting that several motions would make NYSAIS's birth official:

> Moved by Mr. Bradlee, seconded by Mr. Amos that today we set up the nucleus of a State organization.
>
> Moved by Mr. Amos and seconded by Miss Lay (representing Miss Anne Wellington from Emma Willard School) that the name be the New York State Association of Independent Schools.
>
> Moved by Mr. Boocock and seconded by Mr. Meislahn that the membership in this organization shall be limited to those elementary and secondary schools organized under a State charter as non-profit institutions.

Perhaps it's no coincidence that during the same period when the New York State Association of Independent Schools was on its way to the delivery room, a New York City pediatrician and part-time physician at the Brearley School published a book that would become a parenting bible for baby boomers and subsequent generations to come. *Dr. Spock's Baby and Child Care* hit the stands in 1946 and would go on to be translated into over thirty-nine languages and sell over 50 million copies worldwide.[3] As parents and educators can readily attest, having a trusted guide in unfamiliar territory can be a lifesaver. Yet, as the founders of NYSAIS sought to avoid the governmental strictures that plagued the public school system, they had only their courage and their determination to preserve independent school education as an option to help them navigate.

A year and a half would pass before NYSAIS held its first

annual meeting. In between annual meetings, the Executive Committee met twice yearly during May and October, usually at the Albany Academy, to oversee the group's membership and treasury, to plan annual meeting agendas and speakers, and to communicate with the State Department of Education and the National Council of Independent Schools (NCIS). One of the first Executive Committee meetings took place on January 15, 1948, with all co-founders listed in the above letter present. NYSAIS membership now numbered thirty schools, and discussion centered on the growing organization's relationship with the state government and how best to track and respond to pending legislation. Annual membership fees were $10.00 per school, and with expenditures for stationery ($33.75) and the special education service of the New York Legislative Service ($50.00), the treasury balance stood at $216.25.

Perhaps as an outgrowth of the war years—when more than six million women joined the workforce, laboring in factories and farms, serving in the Red Cross and the military—NYSAIS's founders demonstrated some sensitivity to male-female roles in independent schools. In his April 28, 1947 response to President Shafer's initial missive, Morton Snyder, the headmaster of Rye Country Day School, wrote:

> I note that only two ladies are included in the group. Are there not more than two headmistresses in New York State, or even in the metropolitan area, who should be invited to participate?

The role of women in American life would remain an open question for the next several decades. As male veterans returned to the workforce, many women were laid off from their jobs, with the expectation that they would resume their roles as housewives and mothers, surrendering the autonomy and financial independence they had experienced during the war. In 1949, the French author and philosopher Simone de Beauvoir explored the ways that society constrains women's choices and sense of identity in her groundbreaking book, *The Second Sex*, which both anticipated the women's liberation movement and laid an intellectual framework for it.[4]

From its inception, NYSAIS was able to build on the experiences of regional groups who met informally on a regular basis, something that Rye Country Day School Headmaster Snyder mentioned in his 1947 letter:

> I happen at the moment to be Chairman of the "Fairchester Group," an informal organization of a dozen or more private school heads in Westchester, New York, and Fairfield, Connecticut, Counties. I shall attempt to represent this group respectably.

First Annual Meeting

Eighteen months of enthusiastic correspondence and informal meetings finally culminated in the very 1st Annual Meeting of the Association on January 18, 1949 at the Emma Willard School in Troy.[5] The first NYSAIS officers were President Paul Shafer, president of Packer Collegiate Institute; Vice President Anne Wellington, headmistress, Emma Willard School; and Secretary-Treasurer, Harry E. P. Meislahn, headmaster, the Albany Academy. NYSAIS's first guest was Dr. Henry V. Gilson, New York's associate commissioner of education, "who outlined for us some of the plans for legislation and gave us reassurance that where legislation was needed which would affect independent schools, we would be given the opportunity of discussing it with state officials."

The meeting closed with an address by Dr. Francis Parkman, executive secretary of NCIS (which would later become the National Association of Independent Schools, or NAIS), who spoke about "the work of NCIS and of other state organizations similar to ours."[6]

Our infant organization was now cooing and gurgling into the 1950s when popular music was dominated by crooners and ballad tunes, and when the Cold War was also in its infancy. The United States' monopoly on nuclear weapons was broken in 1949 when the Soviet Union tested its first nuclear device, and many in the U.S. government and public perceived that the country was more vulnerable than it had ever been before. Duck-and-cover exercises quickly became a part of Civil Defense drills that every American citizen, from children to the elderly, practiced to be ready in the event of nuclear war. In 1951, during the first big Civil Defense push of the Cold War, the movie *Duck and Cover* was produced (by the Federal Civil Defense Administration) for school showings in 1952. The fear of communism abroad led to the investigation of alleged communists at home, and Senator Joseph McCarthy's anticommunist campaigns and Senate hearings would cast a pall over the first half of the 1950s.

Second Annual Meeting

The 2nd Annual Meeting was held January 17, 1950 at the Emma Willard School, and was attended by twenty-two delegates from member schools and six other representatives or guests. While much of the group's work continued to focus on state regulations, including preparing a "positive proposal to make in the event that the state should initiate legislation designed to control elementary and pre-primary schools which might not meet with the approval of our Association," NYSAIS had also begun to explore establishing its own system for accreditation. At this

A DECADE OF NEWS

Part of NCIS's work was publishing a journal that examined topics of interest to the greater independent school community. The first issue of the *Independent School Bulletin* (which would later become *Independent School* magazine) was published in November 1941. The *Bulletin's* first decade of issues provides a useful snapshot of the nascent national organization and its member schools:

November 1941 *Independent School Bulletin* starts under auspices of Secondary Education Board. Five copies are sent to headmaster or headmistress; additional copies cost 10 cents. The Annual Conference costs 50 cents.

February 1942 "What the Member Schools Are Doing" section

February 1943 "The Granting of Student Aid"

April 1944 "How to Be a Good Trustee"

May 1944 First articles on elementary and preschool education

November 1944 "An Experiment in Teaching Race Relations in a Private School"

May 1945 "Retirement for Teachers"

May 1946 First articles on school finance

November 1946 Conference fee 75 cents

April 1947 First article on teacher training

May 1948 "The Care and Feeding of Audio-Visual Programs"

January 1949 "Colored Students Are an Asset" Conference fee $1.00 "for both days"[7]

same meeting, President Shafer was authorized to contact the Middle States Association (then, the chief organization responsible for accrediting independent schools) to see whether they might undertake an extension of their jurisdiction to include elementary schools.

> Mr. [Folwell] Scull, Headmaster at Poly Prep and former President of the Pennsylvania Association of Independent Schools when he was at Abington Friends School, gave an additional report on accreditation in which he described the methods by which the schools in Pennsylvania arranged to form their own accrediting agency with the permission of the State Board of Education."[8]

French class, Packer Collegiate School, circa 1950

The 1950s saw the rise of a literary movement that was, in part, a reaction to postwar prosperity. The Beat Generation—a term coined by writer Jack Kerouac—challenged American materialism and middle-class values in novels such as Kerouac's *On the Road* and Allen Ginsburg's epic poem *Howl*.

Around this same time a novel about a troubled teenage boy trying to find his way in life was bouncing around the desks of the *New Yorker*, only to find its way to publication in 1951. Written by J. D. Salinger, who was born in New York City in 1919, *The Catcher in the Rye* tells the story of Holden Caulfield, the proverbial boarding school kid and lost soul who finds his way into New York City for a date with Sally Hayes. Here is a brief summary of the book's enchantment and success:

> The *New York Times* ran a review titled "Aw, the World's a Crumby Place" that poked fun at Salinger's style. The *New Yorker* refused to run any excerpts of the novel because they said that the children in it were unbelievably intelligent, and the style of the novel was too "showoffy." But despite the mixed reviews, *The Catcher in the Rye* reached the best-seller list after being in print just two weeks, and it stayed there for more than six months. It has gone on to sell more than 60 million copies. It has been at one time or another both the most banned book in America and one of the most assigned books in American classrooms.[9]

Third Annual Meeting

The 3rd Annual Meeting was held January 16, 1951 at the Albany Academy, with representatives from twenty-five schools present; eight others had sent notice of their inability to attend.

After several invitations to the commissioner of education

and regents chancellor to attend annual meetings, the state continued its noncommittal response by sending the equivalent of a stuffed toy to the baby association. Would this group really amount to anything? Was the state really taking it seriously?

> The minutes of the meeting reflected the state's sentiment: Dr. Shafer asked the secretary to read a very cordial letter from Regents Chancellor John P. Myers regretting his inability to attend our meeting and sending his warm regards to those present with the assurances of the Regents' interest in and cooperation with the problems of independent schools in New York State.[10]

The state's pacifier this time would be Dr. Harry V. Gilson, associate commissioner of education. As recorded in the minutes, "Dr. Gilson extended to the members present the greetings and the regret of Dr. Wilson, Commissioner of Education, in his inability to attend. Dr. Gilson stated his own position with regard to independent schools and spoke for himself in what he believed was the unanimous opinion of the members of the State Department of Education that private independent schools, elementary, secondary, and higher, have a distinct place and function to perform and that education in the United States would be distinctly poorer without them." Dr. Gilson went on to say that the State Board of Regents could not mandate more than half of the high school curriculum, which at that time included four years of English, three units of social studies, one unit of science, and a half unit in health. Interestingly, there was no mention of mathematics.[10]

Dr. Gilson also stated that the department was in favor of schools creating accelerated programs for boys who wanted

◇◇◇

Private independent schools, elementary, secondary, and higher, have a distinct place and function to perform and . . . education in the United States would be distinctly poorer without them.

—Dr. Harry V. Gilson

◇◇◇

to go to college and who otherwise would not be able to do so before becoming eligible for the draft.[10] By this time, fighting around the 38th Parallel in the Korean peninsula was escalating, and in April of 1951 President Truman would relieve the controversial General Douglas McArthur, supreme commander in Korea, of his duties. By the time the Korean War ended in 1953, there were over 36,000 U.S. casualties.

Negotiations and collaboration would continue with the State Department of Education. Dr. Warren Knox, assistant commissioner of education, also spoke at the third annual meeting, emphasizing that it was the state's obligation to keep its schools in "high order." He went on to say "accreditation by special agencies is not applicable in New York State but he indicated his willingness to work with the officers of the Association to formulate such legislation in New York as seems to be needed to protect the children of elementary and sub-elementary age."

Collaboration also continued with Dr. Francis Parkman, executive secretary of NCIS, which was now located in Cambridge, Massachusetts. It was acknowledged that "without a doubt the National Council of Independent Schools has made all independent schools more conscious of problems which schools of their type must face in various sections of the country."[10]

Wilson Parkhill, headmaster of the Collegiate School, "spoke feelingly of the great inspiration Paul Shafer has given our Association in providing it with the impetus which allowed it to move ahead so easily to its present point."[10]

Fourth Annual Meeting

The 4th Annual Meeting was held January 15, 1952 at the Albany Academy, with thirty-nine delegates attending, representing twenty-eight schools. The beginnings of the NYSAIS's collaboration with Catholic schools, another nonpublic school entity, came in the form of "Mr. Charles Tobin, Secretary of the Committee on Catholic Charities, [who] spoke of the mutual interests our Association has with the Catholic group, which represents mutual interests our Association has with the problems of taxation."[11]

Fifth Annual Meeting

The 5th Annual Meeting was held January 20, 1953 at Albany Academy with thirty-six delegates attending, representing twenty-four schools. While the meeting was scheduled to begin promptly at 12 noon, the opening was delayed "so that all delegates could see the United States Presidential Inauguration ceremonies on television in the Albany Academy chapel."[12]

The popular World War II commander (and the former president of Columbia University), General Dwight D. Eisenhower, would now take the place of his commander-in-chief, Harry S. Truman—a transition from Democrats to Republicans. The inaugural parade lasted two and a half hours, and with 22,000 servicemen and women taking part, along with state floats, sixty-five musical units, 350 horses, three elephants, an Alaskan sled dog team, and a 280-millimeter atomic cannon, it "was the most elaborate inaugural pageant ever held."[13]

While Dr. Parkman, executive secretary of NCIS, could not attend, for the first time in NYSAIS history the commissioner of the State Education Department finally attended an annual meeting of the now-toddler association. Commissioner Dr. Lewis A. Wilson stated that 22 percent of the children in this state were now being educated in private and parochial schools.

Out with the pabulum and pacifiers! No longer a toddler, our young association was taking strong, independent steps toward becoming an educational force in the eyes of the state, which had slowly but surely begun to recognize the growing importance of nonpublic schools. The rapid propagation of the new postwar generation was beginning to have an impact on the system.

Dr. Wilson acknowledged the "unbelievable impact" that the baby boom was already having at the elementary school level, and would soon be felt at the junior and senior high levels as well. According to the meeting minutes, he predicted that "if private and parochial schools continue to educate 22 percent of the State's children, we might expect our enrollment to double in the next 10 or 12 years, given a reasonably prosperous era. Our mutual problems are related to financing in view of the effect of inflation. He quoted the National Industrial Conference Index showing that a teacher's salary of $4,000 in 1940 needed to be $5,960 in 1950 to have the same purchasing value. The increase, of course, is reflected not only in salaries, but also in building construction. While 60 percent of children enrolled in public schools do not graduate high school, private schools deal with a more homogeneous group, and do not have the same 'drop-out' problems."[12]

The state director of the division of secondary education called the memorization of factual knowledge the bugaboo of secondary schooling, declaring—in a sentiment familiar to many present-day educators—that too much stress was being placed upon learning for the purpose of passing examinations.

Charles Bradlee, headmaster of Pebble Hill School, cited warnings made at the previous summer's meeting of NCIS in Cambridge, Massachusetts, cautioning independent schools to avoid accepting federal subsidies.

American entertainment and sports were experiencing their own postwar boom. The 1940s and '50s were a golden age for American musical theater, thanks to Rogers and Hammerstein musicals like *Oklahoma!*, *Carousel*, *South Pacific*, *The King and I*, *Flower Drum Song*, and *The Sound of Music*. The team of Lerner and Loewe created two popular Broadway musicals during the 1950s, *Paint Your Wagon* and *My Fair Lady*. Other popular musicals of the 1950s include *Guys and Dolls*, *Peter Pan*, *Damn Yankees*, *The Music Man*, and *West Side Story* among others.[14] Baseball player Jackie Robinson broke the color line with the Brooklyn Dodgers in 1947, and helped the team win the World Series in 1955. Across town, Mickey Mantle joined the Yankees in 1951, won the Triple Crown in 1956, and played in twelve World Series, seven of which the Yankees won.

Sixth Annual Meeting

The 6th Annual Meeting was held January 19, 1954 at the Albany Academy, with twenty-three schools represented. Much discussion at this meeting surrounded nursery school regulation and the tension between the state and independent schools. Mrs. E. J. Thorington of the Elmwood-Franklin School suggested that nursery schools that belonged to established schools should be exempt from whatever regulations were made. She also cautioned that there were many fly-by-night nursery schools that took children away from independent schools, and that independent schools were defeating their own ends because they

◇◇

The memorization of factual knowledge [is] the bugaboo of secondary schooling. Too much stress [is] being placed upon learning for the purpose of passing examinations.

—State Director of the Division of Secondary Education

◇◇

often went their own way and did not have the good of the community at heart.

Later in the meeting, Dr. Parkman from NCIS reported that enrollment was generally up by 2 to 3 percent at member schools; faculty salaries were increasing, although not as rapidly as those for public school teachers; and member schools now numbered 450.

James Allen, deputy commissioner of education, spoke on behalf of the state. He lauded the role of independent schools, saying they "were not restricted by the rules and regulations of public schools; nor did politics interfere with them. They could devote themselves to the thinking processes and were not under so much social pressure. They could remain small and maintain their academic standards, they could seek *quality* in education and stress moral principles."[15]

During this year there was much discussion over a bill in the state legislature requiring registration of any person or school conducting kindergarten or nursery classes. H. G. Ingraham, the counsel representing NYSAIS, provided advice to the association on a regular basis.

Nineteen fifty-four would prove to be an historic year. In Memphis, Tennessee, 19-year-old Elvis Presley made his very first recordings at Sun Records. In less than two years, the whole world would be gyrating to hits like "Hound Dog," "Blue Suede Shoes," "Don't Be Cruel," "Jailhouse Rock," to name a few, and Elvis's impact on pop culture and the baby boom generation would soon become legendary. [16]

But what made 1954 a true milestone was *Brown v. Board of Education*, one of the most seminal court cases in U.S. history. *Brown* had a distinct foundation built on the Thirteenth Amendment (1865), which abolished slavery; the Fourteenth Amendment (1868), which strengthened the legal rights of newly freed slaves; and the Fifteenth Amendment (1870), which prohibited states from denying any man the right to vote due to race. In 1892 an African-American man named Homer Plessy was arrested after refusing to give up his seat on a train to a white man. Plessy decided to fight his arrest in court, and the case eventually went to the Supreme Court. In 1896 the Court ruled against Plessy by a vote of 7-1, enshrining the "separate but equal" doctrine in all areas of public life, including education. But the dissenting opinion in *Plessy v. Ferguson* became a rallying cry for those attempting to abolish the old Jim Crow laws and helped drive one of the most important court cases in the history of U.S. education.

What became known as *Brown v. Board of Education* was actually the name given to five separate cases that were heard by the U.S. Supreme Court concerning the issue of segregation in public schools. Ultimately, the landmark decision declared state laws establishing separate public schools for black and white students unconstitutional. On May 17, 1954, Chief Justice Earl Warren delivered the 9-0 opinion of the Court, stating, "We conclude that in the field of public education the doctrine of 'separate but equal' has no place. Separate educational facilities are inherently unequal . . . ." [17]

Seventh Annual Meeting

The 7th Annual Meeting was held January 18, 1955 at Albany Academy with twenty-five schools represented. Discussion continued to focus on the education of the schools' youngest children, and on efforts to amend state legislation of nursery schools. The word used repeatedly now was "compromise," and ongoing concerns over relations with the state were paramount throughout discussions. It is impressive how much time—volunteer time—was expended by members of the Executive Committee and interested members. [18]

It is interesting to note that the terms "independent schools" and "private schools" were used interchangeably, particularly by state representatives. Such was the case with Dr. F. J. Moffitt, the associate commissioner for elementary and secondary education and that year's guest speaker. According to the minutes, "Dr. Moffitt approached us in a very cordial and friendly way, saying that he saw no conflict, or need for any, between public and Independent Schools. There are 2,000 Independent Schools in New York State and these Schools take care of half a million children. Twenty percent of New York's children are in private and parochial schools. Albany ranks first in its percentage of children in private schools, then come Buffalo, Rochester, New York, and Yonkers. He was proud, he said, of the integrity of our Independent Schools and of the things the Independent Schools do that public schools are unable to do. He hoped to see more and more co-operation between our schools. The State Department [of Education] is there to help us if we need help." [19]

The civil rights movement continued to gain momentum in 1955, when Rosa Parks, exhibiting the same courageous defiance as Homer Plessy, refused to give up her bus seat to a white man, an act that launched the Montgomery, Alabama bus boycott. Nineteen fifty-five also saw the opening of Disneyland in Anaheim, California.

Eighth Annual Meeting

The 8th Annual Meeting was held January 17, 1956 at the Albany Academy. Pertinent items discussed were:

1) The president reported that he had met with Commissioner Allen and had been informed by him that private kindergarten and nursery schools were to be registered on a voluntary basis by the State Education Department.

2) The association debated whether to become an associate member of the College Entrance Examination Board.

3) The association also considered the required number of days in the school year. The state ruling was 175 days, but 160 were deemed acceptable for those schools whose major subjects met five days a week.

4) Dr. Parkman from NCIS reported that he acted as general consultant from independent schools on the White House Committee on Education, and then spoke about the fund started the previous year to help advertise independent schools. He emphasized that "public relations will loom large in our thinking and effort."

5) A group of state officials was in attendance, including the assistant commissioner of education, the director of the division of elementary education, the director of the division of secondary education, and the chief of the bureau of child development. The assistant commissioner of education stated that public and private schools "had a community

of interests and the same basic objectives and New York State was proud of its independent schools."[20]

Ninth Annual Meeting

The 9th Annual Meeting was held January 15, 1957 at the Albany Academy, where it was reported that NCIS had established the Council for Independent School Aid (CISA), its first financial aid program. NCIS set aside $5,000 for the program, and appealed to its member schools to contribute more funds.

At this meeting Dr. William S. Carlson, president of State University of New York, spoke about the university system, including its teacher training programs: the New York State College for Teachers in Albany, which trained secondary school teachers, and the numerous programs dotted around the state for training elementary teachers.[21]

Little did the educators gathered at Albany Academy know that nine months later, on October 4, the Soviet Union would launch an artificial satellite the size of a beach ball and weighing less than 200 pounds. Sputnik 1 became the starting gun for the space race between the Soviet Union and the United States, a marathon that would last well into the 1970s. Within a year's time, the U.S. government passed legislation creating the National Aeronautics and Space Administration (NASA). Sputnik 1's impact on the U.S. education system was sizable, and American schools, concerned that they were trailing their Soviet counterparts, began beefing up their science programs.[22]

Tenth Annual Meeting

The 10th Annual Meeting was held January 21, 1958 at the Albany Academy. "The Chairman introduced for discussion the question of increasing the membership in NYSAIS. It was the sense of the meeting that this matter should be left to the

Executive Committee and that new members be invited to join NYSAIS on a selective invitational basis." NCIS Executive Secretary Francis Parkman reported that "the California Association of Independent Schools had a small representation of schools whereas the Massachusetts Association had a high percentage in the membership. It was Mr. Parkman's judgment that membership should be restricted to school's known to have high standards." [23]

It is important to note that the Executive Committee was charged with making recommendations for school membership: "It was suggested that in the future a full report be made on each school by the Executive Committee before presenting names of schools for action." [23] NYSAIS also voted to join the College Entrance Examination Board (CEEB), with a membership fee of $25. [23]

"Attention was called to the fact that membership in NCIS is now on an individual school basis." [23] Representatives of the association were appointed by the president to attend the NCIS meeting in Cambridge, and the meetings of the CEEB. [24] It was also noted that NCIS would perform special studies to help its member schools and associations. Studies ideas presented included the advanced placement program, the problem of acceleration, study of special courses, alumni/ae funds, faculty salaries, accounting procedures, training for leadership, and mental health. [25]

Contemporary administrators who devote much time and effort to weighing tuition increases will be struck by how casually this information was exchanged at the 1958 meeting: "Mrs. Mason asked for a show of hands on tuition status. Ten schools will increase tuition for 1958-59; thirteen increased tuition in 1957-58; three schools increased tuition in 1957-58 and will further increase tuition in 1958-59." [23]

The chief of the Bureau of Examinations and Testing, State Education Department, stressed the importance of maintaining a good rapport between public and independent schools. He also went on to speak of "the determination of the Regents to keep today's schools in line with today's problems. He cited among other developments the use of T.V. in education and the increased research activity in instruments to measure the quality of instruction. He described the Regents examination as providing a 'uniform yardstick for basic instruction' and said that these examinations are constructed by a representative committee of teachers three times a year. They are recommended for use with other yardsticks to evaluate a program but not dominate it."[23]

"After considerable discussion concerning membership in NYSAIS, it was the sense of the meeting that there not be a membership drive. On the basis of the statement from the annual meeting, the Executive Committee considers the present membership sufficiently representative, but the committee will be glad to consider an application for membership on its merits."[24]

Eleventh Annual Meeting

The 11th Annual Meeting was held January 20, 1959 at the Albany Academy. While time was spent on basic housekeeping—opening a savings account for NYSAIS's growing treasury, which now stood at close to $2,500; the distribution of an NCIS publication on teacher preparation—much of the meeting was given over to a talk by Dr. Warren Knox, New York's assistant commissioner of education. His remarks will sound eerily familiar to contemporary ears: "Dr. Knox in his friendly opening sentences spoke of the good to be derived from independent schools. In his report on New York State Schools, Dr. Knox said,

'Schools in general might have been complacent before Sputnik, but were later not frantic and set about to strengthen the program and thus restored prestige to scholarship!' They got rid of some movements. For instance, not much is now heard about the 'core curriculum.'"

"The Regents Examinations are also under scrutiny in an attempt to set examinations to make sharper discrimination between able and less able students. Certain tests to help identify 'intellectual giftedness' in grades seven, eight and nine will be free of charge to any school. For grades seven–nine the examination is based on the New York state Syllabus. Four subjects five times a week is both 'artificial and inflexible.' The State Department hopes that tests may be used by the colleges."[26]

CHAPTER TWO

Early Childhood Years: 1960s

By 1960, NYSAIS was not only walking and talking, it was expressing itself with increasing confidence, and people—namely the leaders of the State Education Department—were paying attention. Now that it was not merely learning to read, but reading to learn, the association could turn its attention to the wave of baby boom students entering their middle school years—widely considered the most challenging years in a human being's life. Little did the association (or for that matter, the country as a whole) realize that the 1960s would prove to be one of the most challenging periods in modern American history.

By considering just some of the decade's watershed events, one can grasp the breadth of change that took place in ten short years, and the tremendous turmoil that change produced. After the relative calm of the 1950s, who could have foreseen that three major assassinations would make Americans question the fundamental stability of their country? And who could have suspected that a minor conflict unfolding in the then little-known country of Vietnam would further divide the country and claim the lives of more than 58,000 servicemen and women in a thankless, unforgiving war? Yet if the 1960s were often the worst of times, they could also be among the best.

Consider:

- 1961: JFK gives his "man on the moon" speech; the Berlin Wall is built; the Freedom Riders challenge segregation on interstate buses; the Ken doll is introduced; and the Soviets launch the first man in space.
- 1962: The first Wal-Mart opens; Johnny Carson succeeds Jack Paar as host of the "Tonight Show."
- 1963: President Kennedy is assassinated; the first James Bond movie is released; Rev. Martin Luther King delivers his "I Have a Dream" speech at the March on Washington.
- 1964: The Civil Rights Act is passed, ending almost seventy years of Jim Crow segregation in schools, workplaces, and public facilities; Nelson Mandela is imprisoned; Cassius Clay wins his first World Heavyweight Championship.
- 1965: U.S. sends its first combat troops to Vietnam; residents of L.A.'s Watts neighborhood riot in response to decades of discrimination; a massive blackout plunges New York City and much of the Northeast into darkness.
- 1966: Both the Black Panther Party and the National Organization for Women (NOW) are founded; nationwide draft protests are launched.
- 1967: The first successful heart transplant is performed; the Green Bay Packers win the first Super

Bowl; Thurgood Marshall becomes the first African-American appointed to the U.S. Supreme Court.

- 1968: Rev. Martin Luther King and Senator Robert Kennedy are assassinated; U.S. soldiers kill more than 300 Vietnamese civilians in the My Lai Massacre.
- 1969: Neil Armstrong becomes the first man on the moon; the Woodstock festival draws more than 400,000 people for a three-day celebration of rock and roll and the counterculture; the first episode of *Sesame Street* airs; ARPANET, the precursor of the Internet, is established.[1]

One of the most significant changes that independent schools would undergo during this decade can be glimpsed in membership statistics. In the mid-1960s, single-sex schools made up over 60 percent of the NAIS membership; by the mid-1970s, that figure dropped to less than 30 percent, as many single-sex schools went coed, merged with sibling schools, or closed altogether.

As NYSAIS continued to grow and make its presence felt on both the state and national scene, the Executive Committee took on an increasingly crucial role, serving as the mortar that held the association's many building blocks securely in place. As it was for society as a whole, change would be the rule for NYSAIS during the 1960s: changes in the annual meeting's location and format, in personnel, and in organizational structure.

Twelfth Annual Meeting

The 12th Annual Meeting of NYSAIS convened on January 19, 1960 at the Albany Academy to open the new decade for New York independent schools. The tenor of what lay

INDEPENDENT SCHOOL TOPICS

Topics and articles published in *Independent School* magazine give a glimpse of the issues that independent schools were wrestling with in the '60s:

January 1960	"The Care and Feeding of Faculty Wives"
April 1962	The National Council of Independent Schools (NCIS) and the Independent Schools Education Board (ISEB) merge to form the National Association of Independent Schools (NAIS)
April 1963	"A Report on Integration"
October 1965	"Gadgetry in Independent Schools"
December 1965	First article by future NAIS President Peter Relic: "The Battle Against Alienation"
October 1966	"The Vanishing Headmistress" "Mechanization of Data Processing: Part 1: Do You Really Want It?"
February 1967	Annual Conference fee $4.00
November 1967	Cover Theme: Sexuality Education
December 1967	"The Time Is Now: An Integrated Faculty for Independent Schools"
December 1969	Cover Theme: "The Computer as a Teaching/Learning Tool"[2]

ahead was suggested by the meeting's agenda items, most of which touched upon NYSAIS's relations with the state and national education establishment. "As representatives of the Association, Miss [Clemewell] Lay [of the Emma Willard School] and Mr. [Harry] Meislahn [of the Albany Academy] had attended the New York State Teachers Association on Teachers' Education and were impressed by the seriousness and saneness of the discussion." And, Francis Parkman, executive director of NCIS, "illuminated, as always, the workings of his organization, referring to the growth in membership from 15 in the beginning to 30. He reminded us that the purpose of the founding of the constituent members was invariably to meet a threat to the safety of independent schools, that organizations have continued to consolidate their gains and that they now both evaluate themselves and cooperate with the State Government."

A report on the College Entrance Examination Board (CEEB) noted that it is "a rapidly growing organization and truly in the 'Big Business' category; there was a plea for a writing sample on the tests; and a description of the electronic equipment which does 'almost everything.'" [3]

Thirteenth Annual Meeting

At the 13th annual meeting held on January 17, 1961, Cary Potter, assistant executive secretary of NCIS, explained that for the first time NCIS would, on a trial basis, have a representative in Washington, D.C. Just as NYSAIS was doing its due diligence at the state level, NCIS was beginning to make connections within the federal government. [4]

Anthony Terino, chief of the Bureau of Secondary Schools, New York State Department of Education, reported on a small breakthrough in educational television: beginning in September 1961, television station WPIX planned to offer a driver-education course consisting of fifteen half-hour lessons. Terino also discussed the concerns that many independent schools had about accreditation, "fearing that their school year may have to be lengthened and that the curricular requirement of world geography in grade 7 will be forced upon them. He said this is not necessarily so, as the Department uses a formula in working out the required school days because of the relatively longer day in the independent school."[4]

Fourteenth Annual Meeting

One small way to measure the march of progress was the change in the duplication of meeting minutes for the annual meeting held on January 15 and 16, 1962. Instead of carbon copies on onion-skin paper or mimeographed duplicates, the 1962 minutes were printed using a ditto machine (also known as a spirit master, because of the ink's alcoholic content). Every baby boomer can vividly recall picking up a freshly "dittoed" handout from the teacher and inhaling its intoxicating perfume. (While NYSAIS member schools would have to deal with all manner of intoxicants as the 1960s wore on, it's likely NYSAIS switched to this method because the minutes had increased from three pages to ten.)

Another innovation was the introduction of a dinner meeting, which was held at the DeWitt Clinton Hotel in Albany. Dr. Walter Crewson, associate commissioner of education, touched "with wit and wisdom" upon many timely topics, including:

- Local boards of education, which he called the most powerful arm of the American government.
- The attributes of a great teacher: The commissioner of education said that while no one can define what makes a great teacher (and that such greatness is, in

All great teachers transmit aspiration, high ideals, and great thoughts.

—Dr. Walter Crewson, Associate Commissioner of Education

some respects, God-given), all great teachers transmit aspiration, high ideals, and great thoughts.

- The value the Russians place on education: According to our own estimates, the Russians are spending twice as much as we do on education, in proportion to their ability to pay. They apparently think that ideas are the best arsenal in a long-range war, and believe they will ultimately bury us.
- The value that Americans should place on education: Quoting Walter Lippmann, he said that if we are to save our soul as a nation, we must convince people that there is no security in such things as a bank account, a car, or a TV set. We cannot beat the philosophy of Communism without the best schools possible.
- Emergency preparedness: The state would soon issue a brochure on how to construct fallout shelters for use by schools.[5]

The body approved renewing its contract with the New York Legislative Service, the watchdog group that kept NYSAIS abreast of pertinent legislation. Likewise, NCIS's executive secretary reported that it was also reengaging someone to monitor legislation in Washington.

It was during these early childhood years that the association began to find its true independence. Like a youngster learning to ride a bike, NYSAIS discovered it had the ability to manage a group of member schools that all wanted the same thing—to come together as a group, share their collegiality, discuss how to preserve their independence, and all learn together. This development was borne out when NYSAIS held its first two-day meeting, which would help morph the one-day annual meeting into the association's Annual Conference—with a small portion devoted to the annual meeting and the remainder dedicated to collegiality, speakers, and professional development sessions. At this brand-new two-day gathering, Dr. John Jehu, director of the law division, State Department of Education, was the closing keynote speaker. His talk focused on recent legislation of interest to the NYSAIS membership.

Athletics was always important to the association, even in the early years. At the October 31, 1963 Executive Committee meeting, Harry Meislahn reported that as NYSAIS's "on the spot" representative in Albany, he had served as the private school representative on the State Athletic Advisory Committee, which included public, parochial, and private schools.

At its March 2, 1962 Executive Committee meeting, it was noted that as the membership continued to grow, so did the desire to enhance both the programming and location for the annual meetings. The committee determined that "we should devote the evening meeting to independent school problems and keep the morning meeting for our relations with the State of New York."[6] And at the October 31, 1962 committee meeting, it was reported that "The facilities at Albany Academy are being sorely taxed to provide luncheon for the increased membership of the Association. Therefore, alternate places were considered: possibly the hotel, or the University Club."[7]

Fifteenth Annual Meeting

On January 14 and 15, 1963 the annual meeting was held at the DeWitt Clinton Hotel and the Albany Academy. The meeting opened with a dinner keynote speech by Ewald B. Nyquist, deputy commissioner of education, State Education Department. His thirty-two-page remarks, entitled "To Affect the Quality of the Day," concluded with a story that, he said, had special bearing for independent schools:

> I am fond of recalling what Woodrow Wilson, who at the time was President of Princeton University, once said to a mother who brought her boy to Princeton as an entering freshman. She was, oh! so over-solicitous about the welfare of her little boy who was going away from home for the first time. (She was really worried about how they were gong to put two skills into his one skull, or, shall we say, how to keep knowledge from going into one ear and out the other.) She anxiously inquired of a patient and tolerant President, the fortunes with which her darling son would meet in the course of his college career. Woodrow Wilson replied, "Madame, here at Princeton we guarantee success or we return the child."[8]

The Membership Committee was beginning to refine the standards for membership, which was "open to Independent Elementary and Secondary Schools, organized under the Educational Code of the State of New York which shall be represented by the Executive or Authorized Delegate of each school." Other requirements included:

   a) Sponsorship by four member schools;
   b) The school shall have been in existence for five years and the sponsors of the school must be sat-

isfied that the school, both in its organization, objectives, and program, constitutes a sound, independent school;

c) The school should have received its permanent license from the State of New York, and, where applicable, must be accredited by the Middle States Association of Colleges and Secondary Schools;

d) If information about the school appears to the Executive Committee to be inadequate, a visiting committee composed of representatives of member schools will evaluate the applicant, the cost to be borne by the applying school; and

e) The unanimous vote of the Executive Committee, after review of the sponsor's statements. [9]

Also at this meeting, Cary Potter, now the executive secretary of NAIS, reported on the organization's first year of operation. Much of that time had been spent on the mechanical aspects of the merger of NCIS with the Independent Schools Education Board (ISEB). He also reported that the NAIS annual conference would be held in New York on March 1 and 2; that federal legislation and relationships to the national organization would be discussed; and that the pamphlet "Teaching about Communism" had been mailed out to member schools.

Now that the annual meeting was a two-day event, the number of speakers expanded considerably. Along with Dr. Jehu, guest speakers delivered talks on curricular matters, including social studies and foreign languages; advanced placement programs; tobacco use and health services; reading improvement; and registration of schools with the State Department of Education.

As director of the law division of the State Education

Department, Dr. Jehu apprised the assembled of certain anti-segregation laws in place, which made it illegal to deny admission to students on the basis of color, race, or creed. Coincidentally, the association president closed the day with a cautionary note about a member school, which, after rejecting an African-American kindergarten student, received a visit from a committee of the National Association for the Advancement of Colored People (NAACP) and threatened with litigation. While the latter was avoided, the incident was a reminder that segregation had no place in NYSAIS schools.[9]

That same year would see the publication of what would become one of the best-loved children's books of all time: Maurice Sendak's *Where the Wild Things Are*. After young Max causes a big disruption in his house and is sent to his bedroom, he discovers where the wild things are. The book, which won the 1964 Caldecott Medal, might also have been foreshadowing some of the wild things that lay ahead for America, including big-city riots, the escalation of the Vietnam War, and the Northeast Blackout, which left over 30 million people in New York, six other states, and parts of Canada without electricity for up to 13 hours.[10]

But for millions of baby boomers, the biggest news of 1964 was the Beatles' arrival in New York, and their seduction of the country with three performances on "The Ed Sullivan Show" and a pair of concerts at the Washington Coliseum and Carnegie Hall.[11]

Sixteenth Annual Meeting

On January 13 and 14, 1964 the annual meeting was held in Albany. Although forty-five members were expected, only nineteen were able to get to the meeting because of a blizzard, and the business meeting was held at the hotel instead of Albany

◇◇◇

In 1964, there were thirty-four state associations of independent schools, of which NYSAIS was the largest.

—NAIS President John Chandler, Jr.

◇◇◇

Academy. This prompted the group to take stock of a number of issues, including:

- Moving the annual meeting from January to the fall because of the weather.
- Regional associations will play an increasingly important role in the educational world.
- These associations fall into two categories: accrediting and linking.
- NYSAIS has not wished to become involved in accrediting schools, but has made attempts to increase its membership gradually.
- NYSAIS must continue to define its mission, its conditions of membership, and its procedures for promoting its mission among member schools.

In 1964, NAIS President John Chandler, Jr., said there were thirty-four state associations of independent schools, of which NYSAIS was the largest. In all, 110 schools in New York state were NAIS members. He described two popular NAIS publications: a newly revised pamphlet on independent school trustees and a monograph on "The Negro in the Independent School." He also mentioned concerns that prospective NAIS members be screened more carefully, using more specific standards.[12]

Other speakers included Dr. Anthony Terino, chief of the

Bureau of Secondary School Supervision in the State Education Department, who noted some of the challenges confronting schools:

- Poverty: Terino said the education system must prepare people for alleviating economic and cultural deprivation in all parts of the world.
- Increasing enrollment: There were now over 2 million children in New York [secondary] schools, including 70 to 80 thousand in independent schools. As a result, the pupil-teacher ratio had increased and building programs had been stepped up.
- Shortage of qualified teachers: There were too many inexperienced teachers, and too many experienced teachers had been recruited for supervisory and administrative positions before having acquired a sufficient amount of teaching experience.
- Updating the curriculum: It was difficult for school curricula to keep pace with the many rapid changes in the world today.
- Different levels of learners: The State Education Department was wrestling with how to provide for gifted students, while also addressing the needs of slower learners. The State Board of Regents was considering changes to the structure of its examinations that would increase the number of questions for superior pupils to 60 percent, with 40 percent geared for the slower learner.

The final speaker was Phillip J. Moore, an associate in the Division of School Business Management of the State Education Department, who touched on school insurance issues, including fire, property, liability, and automobile.[12]

While 1964 was the final year of the baby boom, this generation that began in 1946 was already causing a logistical nightmare for New York schools. At a special meeting held on October 5 and 6, 1964, Herbert F. Johnson, associate commissioner of Educational Finance and Management Services for the State Education Department, opened with a bevy of often frightening statistics. Here are a few:

- In another twenty years, there would be an additional million schoolchildren in New York state, representing a 40 percent increase.
- The 1965 school population was projected to be 3,180,000. By 1985, it would be 4,391,000, necessitating 48,000 additional classrooms.
- The state population included 1.5 million nonwhites and 2.2 million foreign-born residents.
- The main items in the state education budget remained increased teacher salaries and increased staff. The average teacher's salary throughout the state was now $7,500 ($8,000 in New York City and $7,000 in rural districts).
- The teacher-pupil ratio was 1 to 23.
- Pupils in the state tested one-and-a-half years above the national norms.

Johnson also pointed to larger societal issues that would impact New York schools, including shifting population and migration from farm to city; unemployment; the weakening of personal values; the implications of increased leisure time; the need to achieve equality among all citizens; the general problems of the shrinking world; and the need to understand other peoples.

During the business portion of the meeting, it became

increasingly evident that to keep the organization moving forward, NYSAIS needed to hire a staff person to assist the all-volunteer Executive Committee. NYSAIS President Frank Miller of the Hackley School reported that the Executive Committee had studied the membership form used by the Pennsylvania Association of Private Academic Schools and concluded that "the present set-up of NYSAIS does not provide for processing such a form. It would demand an office and secretary." Further, "the question of an annual report by member schools was referred back to the Executive Committee for further study and the Executive Committee was asked to study the possibility of putting out a brochure for the Association like the one put out by the Northern New England Association of Independent Schools." It is clear that NYSAIS was experiencing the associated growing pains common in the elementary years.[13]

Seventeenth Annual Meeting

The annual meeting was convened on November 16, 1965. Hmmm, November—that seems like the perfect time of the year to have the annual meeting (so much so that NYSAIS has continued to hold all its annual meetings in the fall).

At the opening evening dinner meeting, NAIS President Cary Potter stated that, in his opinion, the involvement of State Departments of Education with independent schools in federal programs was a healthy trend. He also mentioned that with the growth in size of the NAIS national conference, the importance of regional conferences had increased.

The second speaker was Dr. Vincent Barnet, president of Colgate University. After pointing out the rapid rise in college-bound students, as well as the increase in public support for education, he explored the future of the four-year college, particularly private liberal arts colleges. It was the generalist, he said, who would make the decisions about the future of the planet, not the specialist. The independent college must maintain the right to be different, even dangerous, he added, because the main justification for independent education was to be experimental (Colgate itself has an experimental curriculum), and to resist the conformity imposed by bureaucracy. In this way, he stressed, independent education must justify its survival. [14]

At the next morning's meeting, it must have been a surprise when President Miller circulated the new NYSAIS membership application, which had been prepared by the Executive Committee. The purpose of the application was, he explained, "to screen the new members so that the Association is sure that it is composed of good schools. Associations like NYSAIS are going to be pushed into greater activity and will need to speak with authority. They will have the threefold role of defense of member schools, cooperation with the State Board of Education, and cooperation with NAIS." [14]

This was a particularly busy meeting that had many far-reaching items on the agenda:

- The possible evaluation of elementary schools was raised, but no action taken.
- President Miller announced that the Executive Committee had voted to increase the clerical help for the president in view of his more active role.
- This was the first year that the nominating committee would present an officer slate separating the treasurer-secretary office into two separate positions.
- President Miller took up the question of the national assessment program, which was built into the Elementary and Secondary Education Act, 1965. He said that although the tests are not useful to inde-

pendent schools, the state wants some such testing, which would at least provide a statistical picture of the qualifications of independent schoolchildren that might be useful in negotiating with the state. Such tests were, he said, here to stay.

- Harry Meislahn reported on his activities on the Committee on School Safety, Committee on Athletics, working with NYS Public School Athletic Association.

- Gerald LaGrange of Rye Country Day School suggested the use of another hotel.[14]

Other speakers included Irving Ratchick, coordinator of Title I of the Federal Aid to Education Act, and Martin Breck, coordinator for Title II. The former spoke on a program to help fund underserved children, the latter about funding for library materials for schools; both programs would have implications for all schools in the immediate and distant future.

Eighteenth Annual Meeting

The November 14 and 15, 1966 18th annual meeting was held at the Thruway Motel (Exit 24, Albany), and after cocktails and dinner, Dr. Albert E. Holland, president of Hobart College, was the opening speaker. Fifty-eight of the eighty-four member schools were present.

Frank Miller, now the NAIS director of administrative services, reported on the increasingly active role that state associations of independent schools were being asked to take in evaluating elementary schools. He emphasized the vital role of the state associations and their relationship to NAIS.

Three very important items that would impact the future of NYSAIS were addressed: one, passing on expanding member services to NAIS; two, the possibility of evaluating elementary schools; and three, the possible need for a permanent office and a paid executive secretary. While all were in favor of the final item, Harry Meislahn cautioned that the organization should not act precipitously and that some investigation was necessary to find out whether the State Education Department would accept the organization as an accrediting agency and what expenses were involved. [15]

Nineteenth Annual Meeting

The 19th annual meeting of the association was held on November 13 and 14, 1967 at the Schrafft's Motor Inn in Albany. Clinton Dominick, state senator from Newburgh and chairman of both the Senate Education Committee and the Joint Legislative Committee to Revise the Education Law, spoke on the proposed revisions that applied specifically to nonpublic schools.

What made this a particularly critical meeting was that the membership endorsed the Executive Committee's recommendations to proceed immediately to establish a permanent office of executive secretary; to study and institute a dues structure that would support a budget with a present maximum of $20,000, with dues proportional to enrollment (using a formula similar to NAIS); to seek, appoint, and employ an appropriate executive secretary; to determine salaries, duties, location of office, and all other pertinent functions of the secretariat. Also, the Executive Committee recommended that it be authorized to obtain immediately a charter of incorporation for NYSAIS from the Board of Regents.

Information gathered from around the country provided a useful snapshot of what other associations were doing:

- California association: Dues = .5 percent of tuition income; solicits gifts; forty-nine member schools;

budget of $25,000; full-time director and secretary.

- Independent School Association of the Central States (ISACS): Dues = sliding scale by enrollment; income $10,000, plus $2,500 from bulletin; seventy-six members schools; half-time director.
- Southern association: Dues = $15; budget of $3,000; no paid personnel. [16]

Using this data, the Executive Committee created a prospective budget:

- A rough estimate from membership enrollment indicated that dues of .1 percent of members' tuition would produce $35,000.

  o Executive Secretary salary $8,000
  o Part-time secretary $3,000
  o Office rental $1,000
  o Supplies, postage, etc. $1,200
  o Travel allowance $2,000
  o Total budget $15,200

Twentieth Annual Meeting

The 20th annual meeting of the association was called to order on November 12, 1968 at the Schrafft's Motor Inn. President Walter Clark reported on the three Executive Committee meetings that took place throughout the year. A NYSAIS milestone took place on October 25, 1968, when the association was incorporated under a provisional charter granted by the New York State Board of Regents. And he reported that the new executive secretary, Appleton A. Mason, Jr., former headmaster of the Lake Forest Country Day School in Lake Forest, Illinois, was now established in a permanent office in his home at 20 Chestnut Hill North, Loudonville, New York.

With its provisional charter, brand-new executive secre-

◇◇

A NYSAIS milestone took place on October 25, 1968, when the association was incorporated under a provisional charter granted by the New York State Board of Regents.

◇◇

tary, and an office, NYSAIS was, after twenty short years, ready to embrace its autonomy; but a couple of things had to fall into place before that could happen. First of all, its provisional charter required that a constitution and Board of Trustees be put into place, and that is exactly what was voted on during this annual meeting. Of special importance was the NYSAIS Constitution's Article II, which outlined the association's mission:

> The purpose of the organization shall be to promote the independence and well-being of and public regard for the independent schools of the State of New York; to safeguard the interests of these schools in the matter of legislation and regulation; to foster mutually beneficial relations with the New York State Education Department and other educational agencies; to serve as the New York State member association of the National Association of Independent Schools; to assist member schools in maintaining standards of excellence; to encourage activities for the purpose of keeping our education work updated and current; to provide service and leadership to the communities of which we are a part.

Following the election of twelve new trustees, who were well chosen from throughout the state, Executive Secretary Mason discussed some of the ways in which he hoped the association could be of service to member schools.

Individual NYSAIS members reported on a variety of issues:

Exec. Secretary Dr. Appleton Mason

- The association's ongoing relationship with the New York State Athletic Council, on which Meislahn continued to serve.
- The head of the Barnard School for Boys briefly reviewed the strike by fourteen teachers at his school the previous February, which led to a discussion of the possible effects of a teachers' strike on independent schools.
- One member urged schools to obtain accreditation by the Middle States Association of Colleges and Secondary Schools.
- Another member reported on the formation of a new nonprofit organization, the Independent Educational Service, which would supplant the services of the National Teachers Placement Bureau.

Attorneys John R. Titus and Thomas Conneally commented on the implications for independent schools of the Laverne Amendment to the New York State Labor Relations Act, which would become effective on April 1, 1969. The amendment removed the exemption independent schools had formerly received under the Labor Relations Act. Titus made it clear that under the new amendment, heads of schools would be in the same position as other New York employers, and that independent school employees would have all the rights afforded labor under state law, including self-organization and collective bargaining. He went on to urge all schools to contact and begin work immediately with lawyers familiar with labor law, in order to be prepared if and when unionization problems occurred. [17]

Twenty-First Annual Meeting

The close of the decade came with the 21st annual meeting, which was held on November 10 and 11, 1969 at the Thruway Hyatt House in Albany. President Walter Clark announced that instead of Executive Committee meetings serving as the glue between annual meetings, now it would be the Board of Trustees. While the Students for a Democratic Society (SDS) were whipping up dissent on college campuses around the country, New Yorkers had gotten their own firsthand view of campus unrest the previous year when SDS leader Mark Rudd organized a series of student strikes and occupations at Columbia University to protest the university's links to Defense Department think tanks. (Rudd, who also worked to end the draft lottery, went on to form the more radical group the Weather Underground, before going underground in 1970.) Given this upheaval on college campuses, it was no surprise that in his remarks to the annual meeting, John Downing from NAIS singled out two studies sponsored by NAIS: Dr. Otto Kraushaar's study of the American independent school and Allen Blackmer's study on student dissent. [18]

Vice President Stephen Hinrichs of the Harley School and former NYSAIS President Gerald LaGrange led an especially important discussion on state aid for nonpublic schools, which was being considered or was already in effect in forty-seven of the fifty states. As finances became increasingly onerous for the country, the cost of running and maintaining independent schools began to weigh heavily on NYSAIS schools—indeed, on all schools. The next decade would bring even more economic shifts, including the meteoric ascent of gas prices, which would only add to budget pressures schools were experiencing. The heated discussion at this annual meeting reflected the growing pressures:

- "Traditional sources of financial support for the non-public schools may not be adequate in the foreseeable future to assure the continued being of these institutions without a significant diminution in their quality or services."
- "Governmental aid to independent schools will not be acceptable to those schools if acceptance of such aid results in the real limitation of their independence."
- "From the recent survey of 100 schools, [one speaker said] he is aware of a degree of opposition to any form of governmental aid, but he believes that the feeling throughout the country is changing toward a willingness to accept some kind of assistance to solve increasing financial problems."
- "We are in a period of great change, and supporting financial assistance from the State should not seriously limit the independence of a school."
- "Independent schools in Pennsylvania are participating in state aid. On the basis of Pennsylvania law, my school would receive about $50,000 annually."
- "State aid to non-public schools is now a reality throughout the country."

- "When money enters the scene, schools and individuals are inclined to abandon their ideals and principles. We will undoubtedly become involved with [state oversight of] accreditation and the certification of teachers, which will limit a school's independence in selecting faculty."
- "The Catholic Education Association is highly organized, and they have many of the same concerns as independent schools."
- "If aid comes, any school may refuse it, but as an Association we should make it possible for those who are willing to accept aid to do so." [18]

Other topics discussed by the membership included:
- Jackson Bird, chairman of the Elementary School Evaluation Committee, reported the adoption of Elementary School Evaluative Criteria and Standards for NYSAIS.
- Two changes in the bylaws were adopted by the board:
  o The Board of Trustees would now include the immediate past president of the association; and
  o Elementary schools applying for membership must be accredited by the association.
- Executive Secretary Mason reported that he had visited about half the member schools during the 1968-69 school year, and that heads of schools assumed the responsibility for the relationship of their school with the association, rather than delegating this responsibility. [18]

CHAPTER THREE
Elementary Years: 1970s

It was evident by the end of the 1960s that the U.S. had had its fill of the Vietnam conflict. President Nixon had begun to withdraw troops and public pressure to end the war was intensifying. The antiwar protests that had begun on college campuses and spread throughout the country reached a violent climax at the 1968 Democratic National Convention, when Chicago police clashed with antiwar protestors on national television. One of the most potent symbols of the counterculture and its opposition to the war took place the following summer when nearly half a million young people gathered at the Woodstock Festival for what was billed as "three days of peace and music" (along with plenty of drugs).

This message of peace and nonviolence continued to dominate pop music well into the 1970s with songs like "Give Peace a Chance" (The Plastic Ono Band), "Peace Train" (Cat Stevens), "Give Me Love" (George Harrison), "Never Kill Another Man" (Steve Miller Band), "Imagine" (John Lennon), "Man of War"

(The Jacksons), "Some Mother's Son" (The Kinks), and Edwin Starr's venerable "War." As the death toll in Vietnam continued to climb, Americans everywhere asked that same question— "War, what is it good for?"—and pressured Nixon to bring the troops home. The groundbreaking Broadway musical *Hair* likewise captured the exasperation and sadness of the times.

The last U.S. troops withdrew from Vietnam in 1973. That same year saw the start of new international crisis: the Arab oil embargo, when members of the Organization of Petroleum Exporting Countries (OPEC) stopped selling oil to America to protest U.S. support for Israel during the Arab-Israeli war. The embargo led to skyrocketing fuel costs and gas rationing, and people had to sit for hours in their cars, waiting to fill their gas tanks—which they could only do on alternate days, depending on whether their license plate ended with an odd or even number. (In an attempt to circumvent this, I once strapped a gasoline-filled jerry can to the back of my gas-guzzling Gran Torino station wagon and drove from Yuma, Arizona to the Los Angeles airport. Not smart!)

While elementary students feasted on Caldecott Medal–winning books, adults could sort through the turmoil of the 1960s and '70s at the movies, particularly those that depicted conflict in one form or another. (Going to the movies once meant sitting down to a four-course meal—an opening newsreel, the first movie, cartoons, and then the feature film; thanks to the rise of television, by the 1970s going to the movies meant just the feature film.) One particularly popular movie summed up the angst-ridden times when its main character, the news anchor of a struggling network, told viewers over live TV, "I want you to get up right now and go to the window, open it, and stick your head out and yell, 'I'm as mad as hell and I'm not going to take this anymore.'" *Network* went on to win four

TOP MOVIES AND CHILDREN'S BOOKS OF THE 1970S

Films and books reflect the hopes and fears of their times. Consider these popular movies and award-winning children's picture books from the 1970s:

YEAR	OSCAR WINNERS & TOP MOVIES[1]	CALDECOTT MEDAL WINNERS[2]
1970	*Patton; M*A*S*H*	*Sylvester and the Magic Pebble*
1971	*The French Connection*	*A Story A Story*
1972	*The Godfather*	*One Fine Day*
1973	*The Sting; American Graffiti*	*The Funny Little Woman*
1974	*The Godfather: Part II*	*Duffy and the Devil*
1975	*One Flew Over the Cuckoo's Nest*	*Arrow to the Sun*
1976	*Rocky; Network; Taxi Driver*	*Why Mosquitoes Buzz in People's Ears*
1977	*Annie Hall; Saturday Night Fever*	*Ashanti to Zulu: African Traditions*
1978	*The Deer Hunter*	*Noah's Ark*
1979	*Kramer vs. Kramer; Apocalypse Now*	*The Girl Who Loved Wild Horses*

Academy Awards in 1976. (Sadly, Peter Finch, who played the beleaguered anchor, passed away before he could receive his well-earned Best Actor Oscar.)

Twenty-Second Annual Meeting

Upheaval was the order of the day, not only for society as a whole but also for our developing association and the independent school world. The year 1970 saw the breakup of the Beatles, the Kent State shootings, numerous plane hijackings, and the introduction of computer floppy disks. Against this backdrop, the 22nd annual meeting was held on November 9 and 10 at the Thruway Hyatt House in Albany, with sixty-nine member schools, six provisional member schools, one correspondent member school, four guest schools, and nine guests, as noted by board President Stephen Hinrichs.

To better manage this growing membership, the Board of Trustees had met five times throughout the previous year; to better manage its interests with the state, NYSAIS once again employed legal counsel to assist its Legislative Committee as governmental watchdog. Executive Secretary Appleton Mason reported on developments that led toward the present law providing apportionments to nonpublic schools, as well as some of the difficulties in meeting the requirements. At least two-thirds of the membership had decided to make application to the state for payments.

It is interesting to observe the dichotomy that NYSAIS seemed to embrace: acting as a watchdog over state legislation that could affect its members, while simultaneously working to make sure its member schools received applicable state funding in the form of "vouchers, tuition aid, dual enrollment, direct aid, and contract for services." This we-want-it-both-ways philosophy was eloquently addressed by the meeting's keynote

◇◇◇

The general focus of concern is shifting from the question of whether or not there should be an interdependence of the independent school and the State to the question of what form that interdependence should take.

—Gordon M. Ambach, Executive Deputy Commissioner, State Education Department

◇◇◇

speaker, Gordon M. Ambach, executive deputy commissioner of the State Education Department:

> A new relationship [between the state government and independent schools] is not only desirable, but I believe it will be essential to the life of the independent schools throughout the State and throughout the nation. You now have an Albany office with an Executive Secretary. Your discussion this afternoon indicates your increased concern for consciously building a new arrangement, which I can best describe as the interdependence of the independent school and the State. If I may generalize, the general focus of concern is shifting from the question of whether or not there should be an interdependence of the independent school and the State to the question of what form that interdependence should take.

Members also approved three amendments to the bylaws:
1. Increase the number of trustees from twelve to sixteen;
2. Require that new member schools be nonprofit and

admit students without discrimination; and

3. Include a provision that elementary schools may submit an independent evaluation in lieu of an NYSAIS evaluation for accreditation.

Executive Secretary Mason did note that "two schools have been lost as members with the closing of one last June and the consolidation of another"—was this a sign of things to come in the decade ahead? All schools with elementary divisions received copies of the *NYSAIS Evaluative Criteria and Standards*, which had been endorsed by a representative from the State Education Department, who suggested that the statement "Evaluated and accredited for membership in NYSAIS" be used by schools who completed the evaluation process. It was reported that six schools had already been scheduled for evaluation during the current school year. As its own elementary years progressed, the association was already paying more attention to the elementary schools and programs within its membership.

While the annual meeting had traditionally meant conducting business and hosting guest speakers, it was becoming increasingly clear that if the heads of school were going to take two days away from their schools, they wanted to use their time to network with colleagues and learn how they approached running their schools. The 1970 annual meeting introduced panel discussions led by member heads of school, held during the latter part of the conference. That year's annual meeting notes list the following panel topics, along with several salient comments for each:

- Coeducation and Coordinate Education: It was noted that "merger proposals have often had an economic genesis. Single-sex schools may be too small to compete economically or educationally; therefore, some form of cooperation with another school may be essential."

- How to Enlarge the Boarding School Experience: "Boarding schools must be willing to consider and accept many changes to counteract the present alarming attrition rate of 15 percent."

- Senior Year Programs: "Twenty percent of 60 students in the senior class do independent study for half or all year (not just 4 to 6 weeks)."

- Student Government: "Do they simply advise or do they actually have certain powers within the community?"

- Elementary School Evaluation: "Evaluations enable a school to learn its strengths and weaknesses. The self-examination undertaken by the school produces some of the most important values gained from the evaluation. It promotes unification of faculty, students, parents, and trustees, particularly when all groups are represented in the study. The total cost of an evaluation would be about $1,000, but a full-scale evaluation need not be scheduled more frequently than every eight to ten years."[3]

Twenty-Third Annual Meeting

In 1971, the same year that the London Bridge was brought to the U.S., the United Kingdom changed its currency to the decimal system, and VCRs were introduced, the 23rd annual meeting was held on November 15 and 16 at the Thruway Hyatt House in Albany. President Hinrichs introduced the following items for the business portion of the agenda:

- The Elementary Schools Committee had conducted

five evaluations during the year, and five more were scheduled for the remainder of the school year.

- Successful legislative efforts had resulted in blocking compulsory certification for nonpublic school teachers.
- The trustees voted to employ the executive secretary on a full-time basis, thus incurring a deficit budget for 1971-72.[4]

Executive Secretary Mason reported that it was expected that the 1970 Mandated Services Act would continue to provide funds to nonpublic schools. He noted that NYSAIS was meeting regularly with other nonpublic school groups to discuss areas of mutual cooperation. Frank Miller from NAIS reported that the IRS was investigating schools that claimed open enrollment, but did not enroll any black students. Newspaper announcements were accepted as proof of open-enrollment policy. The NAIS boarding school committee reported an increase in empty beds of 1,700 that year.

The annual meeting also offered panel sessions on the following topics:

- Teacher Certification: Kerry Marsh, an attorney and lobbyist who represented the association's interests in the legislature, spoke on state teacher certification policies and alternatives, as well as NYSAIS's position on teacher certification.
- Administration/Trustee/Faculty/Parent/Student/ Alumni—Changing Roles and Relationships: The chairman of the panel posed the opening question, "How do we, and how do others, perceive the roles of responsible members of an independent school constituency?" After acknowledging their lack of

experience in school administration at the time of their appointments, the four heads on the panel suggested that they probably had been chosen as catalysts, on the basis of their potential ability to:

o Manage and bring interest groups together;

o Make good things happen;

o Be supportive of creative energies;

o Deal with other people's problems;

o Draw out talents;

o Share authority while taking responsibility;

o Stand between a person and the mistakes he or she is about to make;

o Be responsive to students' needs to involve themselves in their own learning; and

o Bring faculty into our concern.

- Our Financial Support—New and Changing Sources
- An Experimental High School
- Elementary School Evaluations

Twenty-Fourth Annual Meeting

While in 1972 the Watergate scandal began, swimmer Mark Spitz won seven gold medals and terrorists attacked the Olympic Games in Munich, pocket calculators were introduced, and *M*A*S*H* the television show premiered, the 24th annual meeting was held on November 14 at the Thruway Hyatt House in Albany. President Gerald LaGrange opened the meeting with a reminder that that fall marked the twenty-fifth anniversary of the association.

At the top of the business agenda was an update on the Mandated Services Act. "On November 6, *The New York Times* reported the decision of the Supreme Court to hear further arguments on the Mandated Services Act, which had been declared unconstitutional by a 2-1 vote of the lower federal court in NYC. This action by the Supreme Court was somewhat of a surprise and obviously keeps alive the possibility that the Mandated Services Act may yet provide further funds to the seventy-five member schools of NYSAIS, which participated in this program. The Association was asked to file an amicus brief in support of the several groups which have appealed this case."

The president also reported members' enthusiastic response to the two-day "Quality of Life in a School" workshop held in October for business managers. So began the addition of workshops to the association's repertoire of member services. Members expressed strong interest in additional NYSAIS workshops, including seminars for new teachers, trustees, and a followup on the "Quality of Life" conference.[5]

Twenty-Fifth Annual Meeting

While in 1973 the U.S. pulled out of Vietnam, *Roe v. Wade* legalized abortion in the U.S., Vice President Spiro Agnew resigned, Paul Getty was kidnapped, and the Sears Tower was completed, the 25th annual meeting was held on November 13 and 14 at the Hilton Inn in Tarrytown. President John Skillman of Packer Collegiate Institute reported that the trustees had held five regularly scheduled meetings during the previous year, and that the first evaluation of elementary grades for a K-12 school would be conducted later that year—a practice the trustees endorsed for all schools that had not yet been evaluated at the elementary level. The trustees also offered to provide an informal advisory service to new heads of member schools.

NAIS's director of administrative services reported that the federal government was showing increasing interest in any forms of discrimination in employment practices, especially in which discrimination by sex might be present, including salary

By 1973, the association was focusing increasing attention on providing professional development opportunities for its member schools, a commitment reflected in the establishment of a Professional Development Committee.

differentials. He also noted a number of tax-reform proposals that would severely restrict the contributions of wealthy donors to nonprofit institutions. Independent schools were urged to join in protesting any measures that would seriously curtail or decrease this important source of income.

By 1973, the association was focusing increasing attention on providing professional development opportunities for its member schools, a commitment reflected in the establishment of a Professional Development Committee. Chairman Hinrichs offered the following recommendations:

- NYSAIS should act as a clearinghouse for interesting or innovative programs in member schools.
- NYSAIS should investigate what professional-development assistance NAIS could provide, particularly mini-workshops.
- Regional groups of member schools should be encouraged to organize their own mini-workshop programs.
- Member schools should be encouraged to investigate their local Boards of Cooperative Educational Services (BOCES) programs, particularly book fairs.
- NYSAIS should seek assistance from the Connecticut and Massachusetts associations to develop

workshops similar to their current programs, and should investigate the possibility that NYSAIS teachers in schools located near Connecticut and Massachusetts might attend their workshops.

Another support service the association considered was engaging Austin & Company in Albany to help with property and liability insurances for member schools. Executive Secretary Mason reported that plans for a NYSAIS group major-medical/life insurance program should be completed by January 1. He also made a plea that all member school heads identify themselves to their local state legislators and set up an automatic system for sending letters and telegrams to legislators in times of crisis.

The annual meeting program offered an ambitious, two-day slate of topics, presented by member school heads, administrators, and guests:

- Staff Organization: "Relation of Chiefs to Indians" and "Making Manpower Count."
- Trustee Participation: "Trustees Can Do More Than Trust" and "The Limits of Involvement."
- Developing Teacher Morale: "What Schools Can Do to Make Their Teachers Important" and "What Our Teachers Feel Strongly About."
- The Supervision of Teachers: "Teachers Are Workers, But People, Too" and "Meeting Students' Needs Through Supervision."
- Role of Headmaster in Decision Making: "The Delegation of Power Beyond Guidelines" and "The Buck Stops Somewhere."
- Scales v. Merit: "Fixed Scales, the Only Way" and "I Believe in Merit as the Basis for Salaries."

- Role of the Head in Public Relations
- The Fund Raiser: Internal, External? "The Outside Professional" vs. "The Inside Staff Professional."
- Use of Students in Public Relations [6]

Twenty-Sixth Annual Meeting

The year 1974 saw the resignation of President Nixon, as well as the deposing of Emperor Haile Selassie of Ethiopia, the defection of Soviet dancer Mikhail Baryshnikov, and the kidnapping of Patty Hearst. The 26th annual meeting was held on November 12 and 13 at the Hilton Inn in Tarrytown, and boasted the largest turnout for an annual meeting in the association's history. Representatives from 85 percent of the member schools were in attendance, including 79 percent of the school heads, for a total of nearly 200 participants.

President Skillman noted that NYSAIS trustees had met four times during the year, and pointed out that having an executive secretary continued to bring added organization and professionalism to the association. Executive Secretary Mason once again urged all schools to develop lines of communication with their state senators and assemblymen, because those connections would be important during the 1975 legislative session. The business meeting included a review of insurance coverage options and professional development programs, and was followed by a special interest session on school evaluations by the Middle States Association of Colleges and Secondary Schools, and a keynote address by Ewald B. Nyquist, commissioner of education, the University of the State of New York. Panel discussions included:

- Fund Raising in a Down Market
- Faculty Participation in Establishing Salary Levels
- Effective Management in Independent Schools

- Women and Education: "Images of Boys and Girls in Children's Literature and One Woman's Aspirations"
- What Happens When You Integrate
- Student Filmmaking
- Alternative Forms of Education: "Causes and Consequences"
- New Concerns in Physical Education for Independent Schools
- Learning Disabilities: "Identification and Remediation" [7]

Twenty-Seventh Annual Meeting

In 1975 Pol Pot and the Khmer Rouge came to power in Cambodia, unleashing a genocide that would claim the lives of one in four Cambodians. In that same year, civil war broke out in Lebanon, Microsoft was founded, Arthur Ashe became the first black man to win Wimbledon, and the 27th annual meeting was held on November 5 and 6 at the Hilton Inn in Tarrytown—a venue that would serve as the meeting's home for the next several years. President Richard Barter of Collegiate School began the meeting by describing the various activities of the trustees during the past year. He urged support of the Association of Teachers of Independent Schools (ATIS) Book Fair on February 6, 1976 and reported on the efforts of Meredith Minz of the Calhoun School to develop useful information concerning Title IV programs as they pertained to independent schools. He also urged member schools to contact the executive secretary if they encountered difficulties meeting State Education Department regulations.

The association's growing confidence about its role was evident in Executive Secretary Mason's remarks to the membership regarding the differences in public and nonpublic education. "He reported on a presentation by the Conference for Nonpublic Education at the Board of Regents Annual Legislative Conference in September. The presentation expressed concern regarding the increasing trend to impose public school standards and regulations on nonpublic schools. Some state officials seem to be losing sight of the fact that nonpublic schools are different from public schools and that many regulations appropriate for public schools are inappropriate or even detrimental to nonpublic institutions. It was important, however, for independent schools to resist the type of regulation that did not have a legal basis and which should not be required of our schools."

With the theme of "The Changing Independent School World," the annual meeting's discussions, keynotes, and panels included:

- Opening Session: "What Will It Mean to be an Educated Person in Tomorrow's World?" by Dr. Robert F. Bundy
- A presentation by the Educational Records Bureau (ERB)
- "Applications of Computer Technology for Independent Schools" by Shared Educational Computer System
- "Laws, Regulations, and the Courts: Some Changing Issues School Heads and Trustees Should Be Thinking About"
- "The Teaching and Learning of Values"
- "Communications in the Changing World of Independent Schools" by Richard L. Brecker, President of Brecker & Merryman
- "Recruitment by Independent Schools: Market Surveys and Public Relations"

- "The Changing Role of an Independent School Business Manager: The Relationship Between the Head of School and Business Manager and What Each Should Expect From the Other"
- "Teacher Evaluation"[8]

Twenty-Eighth Annual Meeting

While America celebrated its bicentennial in 1976, elsewhere North and South Vietnam joined to form the Socialist Republic of Vietnam, the first Ebola virus outbreaks struck Sudan and Zaire, China's Tangshan earthquake killed over 240,000 people, and gymnast Nadia Comaneci scored seven perfect tens at the Summer Olympics. The 28th annual meeting was held on November 9 and 10 at the Hilton Inn in Tarrytown. As soon as President Barter convened and welcomed the members, he asked for a motion to adopt the newly revised bylaws, which subsequently passed unanimously. At this point in the evolution of the association, its purpose continued to be clear and well focused, as reflected in the newly adopted bylaws:

> The purpose of the corporation shall be to promote the independence and well being of and public regard for the independent schools of the State of New York; to safeguard the interests of these schools in the matter of legislation and regulation; to foster mutually beneficial relations with the New York State Education Department and other educational agencies; to serve as the New York State member association of the National Association of Independent Schools; to assist member schools in maintaining standards of excellence; to exchange information about new educational or administrative methods and practices; to encourage activities for the

NYSAIS NEW YORK STATE ASSOCIATION OF INDEPENDENT SCHOOLS
20 CHESTNUT HILL NORTH, LOUDONVILLE, N. Y. 12211 — (518) 463-0240

APPLETON A. MASON, JR.
    EXECUTIVE SECRETARY

Letterhead, circa 1976

purpose of keeping the schools' educational curricula current; to provide service and leadership to the communities of which the schools are a part.

At the close of the business meeting, Barter announced that Stephen Hinrichs, headmaster of the Harley School in Rochester, would become the new executive secretary of NYSAIS.

As the association became more sophisticated in its purpose and organization, so did the programs it offered its membership. Here is a sample of the speakers, panels, and topics presented in 1976:

- "The Educational Impact of Miniaturization of Computers," with panelist Seymour Papert, professor at MIT
- Reorganization of NAIS, with panelist W. Rodman Snelling, headmaster of the Tatnall School
- "Strategies for the Continuing Education of Teachers," with panelist Peter V. Buttenheim, associate director of the Graduate Liberal Studies Program at Wesleyan University
- "The Education and Inspiration of the Board of Trustees"
- "The Education and Enlistment of the Parent Body"[9]

At the same time, NYSAIS's vigilance in keeping the state government at bay was one of the behind-the-scenes services that meant so much to its members. Here is a perfect example of how the Board of Trustees employed its executive secretary in 1976 to oversee any and all governmental intrusions:

> Mr. Mason reported on the proposals of the Commissioner's Task Force on Teacher Certification which would require an examination and licensing for all teachers in the State. NYSAIS is joining with other nonpublic schools in opposing this proposal. There is a strong likelihood of legislation to be introduced by the teacher unions to effect their goals. It was the sense of the meeting that NYSAIS should continue to oppose such proposals in vigorous fashion. If action by the membership is required before Feb. 16, the Executive Committee was empowered to consider the necessary forms it should take. [10]

During this same period, NYSAIS was working more and more with the New York State Council of Catholic School Superintendents on behalf of all the state's nonpublic schools. On November 11, 1976, Mason and the council's executive secretary spoke to the New York State Task Force on Teacher Education and Certification, representing over 600,000 students and approximately 35,000 teachers. Here are excerpts from their very direct statement to the assembled body:

> While we applaud the primary goal of seeking ways to improve the quality of teaching in New York State, we note with dismay and disbelief an underlying assumption made by the Task Force report that public schools and nonpublic schools are not significantly different. It could only be through such a misconception that the

recommendation was made to include nonpublic school teachers in a teacher examination and licensing program designed on the basis of public school teaching. Further, it must have only been through such a misconception that the Task Force felt qualified to make such a recommendation when the Committee includes not a single representative of nonpublic elementary and secondary schools or teachers.

NYSAIS protested that a proposed state-run teacher certification program had "offended nonpublic education in attempting once again to force nonpublic schools into the Procrustean bed of the public school model." [11]

Twenty-Ninth Annual Conference

With this eloquent defense of independent education, the almost-adolescent association was vigorously fulfilling its mission "to safeguard the interests of these schools in the matter of legislation and regulation," and well serving its 100-school membership. Nineteen seventy-six was a pivotal year in establishing the association among its nonpublic school peers and in the halls of the state education and legislative establishment.

While in 1977 Elvis Presley was found dead, the South African anti-apartheid leader Steve Biko was tortured to death, the TV miniseries *Roots* aired, and the first *Star Wars* movie was released, the 29th annual meeting—now called the annual *conference*—was held on November 3 and 4 at the Hilton Inn in Tarrytown.

Even in the elementary years of its existence, NYSAIS was viewed by its members as a New-York-City-centric association. Understandably so: By the mid-1970s, roughly thirty-six of the 100 member schools hailed from the city. Every once in a while it was made known—quietly and otherwise—that a preponderance of association activities, including board meetings, were held in the city. One of the more overt examples came when Stephen Hinrichs, in his newly appointed role as executive director and sporting NYSAIS's brand-new letterhead, penned a letter dated March 29, 1977 to the trustees regarding the board's upcoming meeting on May 3. Here is an excerpt from that letter:

THE NEW YORK STATE ASSOCIATION OF INDEPENDENT SCHOOLS
33 WARDER DRIVE, PITTSFORD, NEW YORK 14534   716-586-2637

STEPHEN HINRICHS   *EXECUTIVE DIRECTOR*

Realizing that you can hardly contain your excitement at the prospect of a trustees' meeting in the Western Lake Country, we make haste to post to you the salient facts you will need for your planning.

You should know first that no visa is necessary. While New York City still withholds diplomatic recognition from the western provinces, all restrictions on travel have been removed. The threat that the Oneidas will exercise their claims to traditional hunting grounds remains real but should prove no obstacle to passage. Predictions for a warm spring should assure no more than a modest residue of snow. Incidentally, reports of a return to the ice age to this region have been examined and found without substance.

For the benefit of those whose geographic ignorance leads them to conclude that all cities west of Albany are named Buffalo (viz., Hume and Mason), this meeting will be held in Rochester, a modest collection of artisans' cottages on the banks of the Genesee. The natives are cautious but friendly. Some even speak a form of English.

Hinrichs also apprised the trustees of the need to upgrade the NYSAIS office with the purchase of a new typewriter, a simple copier, and some essential office furniture—a sign of the association's growing professionalism and stature in the independent school world.

At the national level, single-sex schools made up over 60 percent of the NAIS membership in the mid-1960s; by 1978, that figure had dropped to just 28 percent.

Stephen Hinrichs, board president and second executive director

In Congress, New York Senator Daniel Patrick Moynihan sponsored a bill in defense of private education and tuition credits, and spoke about this legislation at the NAIS Annual Conference. Organizationally, NAIS had chosen to work with existing state and regional associations, instead of replacing them in part with regional NAIS offices. But NAIS's decision not to relocate its headquarters from Boston to Washington left "many New York [school] heads unpersuaded that their voice has been heard [in Congress]. Trustees instructed President [David] Hume [of St. David's School] and the executive director to draft a letter to NAIS President Jean Miller (cc to Potter and Kast) stressing the importance of actual and symbolic focus on Washington and consideration of this mandate in the selection of the next NAIS President." [12]

Mohonk Mountain House

Thirtieth Annual Conference

While in 1978 the first test-tube baby was born, John Paul II became pope, and Sony introduced the Walkman, the first portable stereo, the 30th annual conference was held on November 2 and 3 at the Mohonk Mountain House in New Paltz, with 159 attendees representing eighty member schools and related organizations. But it was the news that followed a few weeks later on November 18 that would rock the foundation of every educator: the Jonestown Massacre, a mass murder-suicide orchestrated by People's Temple cult leader Jim Jones in his "promised land" compound in Guyana. Of the 918 people who died, 304 were children. [13]

Throughout the course of this year, many important matters were resolved, not the least of which was finding a new permanent home at Mohonk Mountain House for the association's annual conference. On January 18, 1978 Hinrichs reported to the trustees that the 1977 annual conference realized revenues of $3,337.25 and expenses of $3,320.22, for a net profit of $17.03.

At the March 1 Board of Trustees meeting, the Elementary Schools Committee reported that the evaluation of K-12 schools was being considered, and that there appeared to be merit in holding a single evaluation for an entire school, rather than a NYSAIS evaluation of the elementary school and a Middle States evaluation of the secondary level. The committee expressed concern about those K-12 schools that were accredited by the Middle States Association but had not taken advantage of the opportunity of a voluntary evaluation of the elementary grades. [14]

President Hume reported that NAIS intended to divide the Mid-Atlantic Region and create an East Region made up of New York and New Jersey, which could elect two area directors to NAIS by methods of their own choosing. At the same meeting, the board approved a special committee to study alternatives for the evaluation of NYSAIS member schools. Joan McMenamin of the Nightingale-Bamford School reported on planning for the next annual meeting, and it was suggested that she and the executive director use as a departure point a recent NAIS publication on the evaluation of trustees and heads. It was agreed that the presence of State Education Commissioner Gordon Ambach as keynote speaker would support a key conference objective, that of enlarging the understanding between the independent schools and the State Education Department. [15]

Balanced budgets and growing reserves prompted the trustees to set up an investment fund with E. F. Hutton. The trustees also continued to refine and formalize the accreditation process, as this excerpt from the minutes of their September 27, 1978 meeting indicates: "The Executive Director proposed a procedural change in order to expedite the returning of the evaluation report to the school evaluated. He recommended that the Chairman of the Evaluation Visiting Committee present the final report to the Committee on Evaluation and Accreditation, which will review the report and release it along with the rated criteria to the school as soon as possible in order to maximize the effectiveness of the visitation. Formal approval of the evaluation report continues to be the responsibility of the full board of trustees."

Also reported was the formation of the NYSAIS Scholarship Fund for the distributing of foundation, corporate, and private contributions to support scholarship programs at member schools. The M. Kaplan Fund of New York pledged an initial $25,000. The meeting closed on a personal note, when President Hume presented the executive director with a customized weathervane—a miniature replica of his boat, the *Tetra*—as "a belated but fitting wedding gift from the trustees to Mr. and Mrs. Hinrichs." [16]

It was reported to the trustees that while the NYSAIS Athletic Association could not be formally approved by the membership until the annual meeting, the Federation of Athletic Associations had recognized the NYSAIS Athletic Association as the sole representative of the state's private schools. (On November 2 at the annual conference the New York State Independent Schools Athletic Association was approved and its constitution was adopted.) [17]

Thirty-First Annual Conference

While in 1979 the Ayatollah Khomeini returned from exile to become leader of Iran and fifty-two Americans were subsequently taken hostage in Tehran, Margaret Thatcher was elected the first female prime minister of Great Britain, Mother Teresa was awarded the Nobel Peace Prize, and a nuclear accident took place at Three Mile Island. That same year the 31st annual conference was held on November 1 and 2 at Mohonk Mountain House, New Paltz.

Earlier that year at their January 19 meeting, the board of trustees adopted the procedure that "all applications for membership would now go through the executive director, who would investigate the applicant, examine documents submitted and conduct a visitation of the school's premises, assign a preliminary classification, and make a report to the Membership Committee." At the same meeting the following motion was moved and approved by the trustees:

> The New York State Association of Independent Schools Trustees feel it is important for its Athletic Association to exercise its responsibility to participate in the formulation and implementation of policy by the Federation [of Athletic Associations]. We, therefore, resolve that the New York State Association of Independent Schools is opposed in principle to post-season, state-wide athletic tournaments, as such activities are inconsistent with our schools' philosophy regarding the role of athletics. We recognize the right of individual schools to make independent decisions.

At the same meeting Hinrichs reported that he had solicited 178 foundations on behalf of the NYSAIS Scholarship Fund: thirty-two responses had been received, twenty-six refusing participation, two returned because of no forwarding address, and four responses meriting further exploration. The Committee on the Scholarship Fund met following the board meeting to define the terms of the grants.

At its June 13 meeting, much of the board's discussion surrounded better coordination with Middle States Association, and school evaluation and accreditation approvals. The trustees also made special note of their "admiration, affection, and support for their Executive Director," particularly for "his qualities of expertise and wisdom as a retired head in the support he extends to members of our community."

As we come to the close of the association's elementary years and look ahead to the preadolescent "tween" years, it is important to reflect on NYSAIS's momentous growth to date. Not unlike the elementary years of any child, this rapid growth—physical, social, and intellectual—was necessary to prepare for the daunting preadolescent and adolescent years still to come. As we will see, the solid foundation assembled in the first three decades would prove to be instrumental for the continued vitality and productivity of not only the association but also the many member schools it serves. This commitment to the association's long-term development is evident in an excerpt from the minutes of the June 13 board meeting:

> A long discussion was held concerning the future of NYSAIS in the coming years and beyond. We reiterated our desire to put the special dimensions of our Executive Director at the service of Board Chairmen and Trustees, as well as the other principal executive and administrative officers of our schools. We discussed the possibility of gathering area schools for meetings with Hinrichs, agreeing that we wished no more than 8 to 10 schools at one meeting.

CHAPTER FOUR

Preadolescent Years: 1980s

The tween years for any child can be mysterious and unsettling, yet also fulfilling and rewarding, punctuated by a bounding curiosity and a fervent desire to learn and become more adult-like. Contemplating an infinite array of experiences on the horizon, a preadolescent child is changing socially and physically. Likewise, by the 1980s, our association was primed for growth and ready to come into its own in the independent school world.

The best part of chronicling NYSAIS's growth is the fact that, starting in the middle of this decade, I got to observe it firsthand from my position as an assistant head of school, living and working on the North Shore of Long Island. This good fortune allows me to dispense with the year-by-year diary format of the first three chapters, and present the association's history in a more story-like fashion. While I will still draw upon trustee meeting minutes, executive director and staff reports, newsletters, and quotes, the history of NYSAIS will be enriched with personal interviews conducted expressly for this book.

Stories help us better understand our history. Classic portraits of New York history—such as David McCullough's *The Great Bridge*, Robert Caro's *The Power Broker*, Betty Smith's *A Tree Grows in Brooklyn*, Claude Brown's *Manchild in the Promised Land*, and E. B. White's *Here is New York*—immerse us more fully in historical events because they tell us the stories behind those events. Alex Haley, Madeleine L'Engle, Herman Melville, Joyce Carol Oates, and James Baldwin are but a few of

BEST CHILDREN'S BOOKS OF THE 1980s

NEWBERY MEDAL WINNERS[1]
1980 *A Gathering of Days: A New England Girl's Journal, 1830-1832* by Joan W. Blos
1981 *Jacob Have I Loved* by Katherine Paterson
1982 *A Visit to William Blake's Inn: Poems for Innocent and Experienced Travelers* by Nancy Willard
1983 *Dicey's Song* by Cynthia Voigt
1984 *Dear Mr. Henshaw* by Beverly Cleary
1985 *The Hero and the Crown* by Robin McKinley
1986 *Sarah, Plain and Tall* by Patricia MacLachlan
1987 *The Whipping Boy* by Sid Fleischman
1988 *Lincoln: A Photobiography* by Russell Freedman
1989 *Joyful Noise: Poems for Two Voices* by Paul Fleischman

ADULT BESTSELLERS OF THE 1980S

BESTSELLING NONFICTION[2]/ FICTION[3]

1980 *Cosmos* by Carl Sagan / *The Bourne Identity* by Robert Ludlum

1981 *A Light in the Attic* by Shel Silverstein / *Gorky Park* by Martin Cruz Smith

1982 *Jane Fonda's Workout Book* by Jane Fonda / *Space* by James Michener

1983 *Motherhood: The Second Oldest Profession* by Erma Bombeck / *The Name of the Rose* by Umberto Eco

1984 *Mayor* by Edward Koch and William Rauch / *First Among Equals* by Jeffrey Archer

1985 *A Passion for Excellence* by Tom Peters and Nancy Austin / *The Cider House Rules* by John Irving

1986 *Fatherhood* by Bill Cosby / *Red Storm Rising* by Tom Clancy

1987 *The Closing of the American Mind* by Allan Bloom / *Misery* by Stephen King

1988 *Trump: The Art of the Deal* by Donald Trump and Tony Schwartz / *The Bonfire of the Vanities* by Tom Wolfe

1989 *All I Really Need to Know I Learned in Kindergarten* by Robert Fulghum / *The Satanic Verses* by Salman Rushdie

the notable authors born in New York who shared their stories and experiences from a New York perspective.

The new decade found the trustees and Executive Director Stephen Hinrichs struggling with five major issues:

1. Managing the evaluation and accreditation process;
2. Satisfying State Education Department (SED) requirements for accreditation and athletics;
3. Determining how to deal with for-profit schools as members;
4. Establishing an education program for school trustees; and
5. Addressing the increasing need for more support staff to administer the growing needs of the association, so that it could better serve its member schools.

At one of their first meetings, Hinrichs "commented on the various courses in evaluation and accreditation NYSAIS might take and how these might affect our relations with the Middle States Association, the State Education Departments, and NAIS. Discussion followed." Compromise was the best solution for keeping all entities satisfied and maintaining high quality within member schools. The trustees' recommendations will sound familiar to those familiar with the school accreditation process:

- Under the auspices of NYSAIS, member independent schools (and any others who may so request) will, at intervals no greater than 10 years, undertake full self-evaluations using an approved manual or criteria and the SED "Guide For the Review of Non-Public Secondary School Programs."
- Following the self-evaluation, schools will be visited

for three days by a committee chaired by an independent school head and including a representative
of the State Education Department and at least one
public school member.

- The self-evaluation and the visit will, on the recommendation of the visiting committee to the Assistant Commissioner for Non-public Schools and the governing
body of NYSAIS, lead to registration by the State (in
the case of schools including secondary grades) and
accreditation by NAIS acting through NYSAIS.

- The present requirement of annual reports to the
SED, NAIS, and NYSAIS will be continued.

- Schools which wish to continue their present affiliation with Middle States or to initiate such an affiliation
will not be discouraged. The proposal by NYSAIS is
offered as an option, not a requirement.[4]

A survey conducted by the association's Committee on
Accreditation and Evaluation found that of the eighty-nine
schools responding, twenty-three schools planned to continue
to be evaluated by the Middle States Association, while the
remaining sixty-six would either continue or begin to be evaluated by NYSAIS.[5]

Meanwhile, the NYSAIS Athletic Association found itself
playing a similar game with the State Federation Athletic Association regarding tournament play and age-eligibility requirements. It is evident by the accreditation course of action taken
and the athletics requirements exercised between NYSAIS and
the state that the association was still intertwined with the State
Education Department (and NAIS). Full independence would
take a bit more time.

One other struggle that continued to plague the association was how to deal with proprietary or for-profit schools that wished to become members of NYSAIS, and a subcommittee was formed to study the matter further.

At the April 16 board meeting, Hinrichs reported that "it was recommended [proprietary schools] not be admitted because lobbying in the name of non-profit schools would be complicated, the public image of the association might suffer, fund raising would be compromised, other joint endeavors assuming non-profit status would be damaged."

The struggle to educate school boards on good governance would, over the course of the decade, culminate in a program administered by a NYSAIS Trustee Committee and staffed by the executive director. The proper role of school boards was to ensure school stability and provide appropriate support to the head of school. With those goals in mind, the trustees established an elaborate committee to study and design a program to educate and train school board members.

The trustees also began to consider principles of good practice for teacher recruitment and hiring and for student enrollment. Drafted by Trustee Fred Withington of Friends Academy and presented to the board in June 1981, the "Principles of Good Practice Governing the Recruitment of Teachers" was adopted.

Hinrichs informed the board that the association office would move to Canandaigua during the summer of 1981. Relocation continued to be a topic for NAIS as well. In a letter from NAIS President John Esty to association executives and presidents, he stated that discussions continued about moving NAIS offices from Boston to Washington, D.C. to best represent its 1,200 member schools with the federal government.

All these ambitious efforts—administering a strong accreditation and evaluation system, while also managing a growing membership and providing an increasing number of services—

placed large demands on NYSAIS's small staff. Hinrichs helped the NYSAIS trustees understand the necessity of providing sufficient resources for administering those programs they chose to undertake.[6] Accordingly, in January 1982 Joan Reed was hired as an associate in the NYSAIS office.

Member services continued to grow, often in response to member requests. For example, an inquiry by Trustee Gordon Clem of St. Thomas Choir School about establishing a committee on teacher services led the board to announce, at its April 21, 1982 meeting, that the Beginning Teachers Institute (BTI) would be held October 31 through November 2 that year. (Clem's request that the association form a committee on minority affairs was not immediately acted upon.) Also scheduled that same year was the Business Affairs Conference, which attracted 130 registrants. Trustee workshops gained momentum, with four scheduled throughout the state during October 1982.[7, 8]

At a regularly scheduled board meeting, trustees held a brainstorming session to consider topics that might be presented at the 1983 NYSAIS annual meeting. Those topics provide a window on member concerns and the issues of the day:

- The values that underlie our schools;
- The issue of nuclear power: both the risks of exposure and the campaign for nuclear disarmament;
- Technology and values, and technical developments that have moral implications;
- Institutional leadership; and
- The philosophy of compensation.

The board was confronted with a number of issues related to accreditation: the association's relationship with the Middle States Association; public school personnel sitting on NYSAIS visiting committees; visiting chairs being asked to visit schools a year in advance; and the many other demands upon the executive director, which prevented him from being able to spend more time on school evaluations.[9]

The buzz at the 1983 annual meeting centered on how independent schools should respond to the New York State Regents' Action Plan. What ways, for instance, could NYSAIS schools demonstrate outcomes (i.e., ERBs, SATs)? Part of the problem, from the association's perspective, was that individual regents did not understand the differences between public and independent schools. While Assistant Commissioner Joan Arnold spoke and provided some context for the Action Plan, further discussion led to three proposed courses of action:

- Question the constitutionality of the Regents' Plan;
- Cooperate with the public sector and try to defend the freedom of our NYSAIS schools; and/or
- Seek exception from the Regents' proposals.[10]

One of the first interviews I conducted for this book was with Fred Calder, who served as NYSAIS's executive director from 1986 to 2007. He vividly recalled a contentious meeting from this period with State Education Department officials:

> One particular commissioner was not exactly threatening, but strongly suggesting that we, as independent schools, should start giving these tests and all that [bleep] that they were doing in the Regents' exams they had set up. And that we [NYSAIS] were registered by the Regents, which theoretically was what gave us the power to grant diplomas. So there was a suggestion in this meeting that, "You know, if you don't shape up, then [the Regents] could start taking your registration away." At that point, I rose out of my seat. I said, "Commissioner, if the Depart-

ment of Education ever starts deregistering some of the most powerful academic schools in the United States, it's going to be a combination of *Alice in Wonderland* and Franz Kafka." And there was this, this silence.[11]

Calder added that this story was a favorite of Tom Hogan's, a close ally who worked in the State Education Department's Office for the Commissioner for Nonpublic Schools from 1982 to 2010. Calder urged me to speak with Hogan as well: "He's got a lot of experience with accreditation, and he also helped incorporate independent schools and dealt with charter problems."

I had an opportunity to interview Tom Hogan on April 21, 2014, and just as Calder said, Hogan was a wonderful asset to nonpublic schools. Whether serving as an intermediary or keeping a watchful eye on legislation on behalf of nonpublic schools (including NYSAIS members), he was always willing to help NYSAIS executive directors advocate for independent schools with the State Education Department. Hogan mentioned that by the time he retired, there were a number of nonpublic school organizations representing their respective constituencies, including Jewish, Lutheran, Catholic, and Islamic associations, as well as NYSAIS. The cumulative effect of all of these organizations gave added strength to each individual voice.[12]

While the great social upheavals of the 1960s had begun to subside by the 1980s, a new and unforeseen threat cast a long shadow over the decade: the AIDS epidemic. The very first cases of what would become known as AIDS were diagnosed in 1981; by the close of the decade, 100,000 cases had been diagnosed, largely among young gay men and intravenous drug users, and the mortality rate was climbing toward 10,000. I distinctly remember reading Randy Shilts' book *And the Band Played On* (St. Martin's Press, 1987) because, as a middle school "sex-ed"

teacher, I wanted to learn all that I could about this disease that was ravaging so many lives so fast.

What really struck home was when I attended a CRIS (Council for Religion in Independent Schools) conference and heard the Reverend Roger Bowen, then the chaplain at St. Albans School in Washington, D.C., talk about how his school community had rallied around—rather than ostracized—Vaughn Keith, a classics teacher who contracted AIDS and died. Keith's obituary includes a poignant quote from the Reverend Mark Mullin, St. Albans' headmaster: "The parents and students were extremely supportive. No one withdrew from the school. No one withdrew from his classes. It gave him an important mission in living. The boys could see the dangers of this disease. AIDS had always been something that happened to someone else." [13]

The gains of the 1960s civil rights era did not mean an end to racial tensions. In New York City, anxieties about rising crime rates contributed to several high-profile racial incidents, including the December 22, 1984 shooting by Bernhard Goetz of four African-American teenagers who had allegedly accosted him on the subway. Goetz was hailed as a hero by some and denounced as a vigilante by others; although he was initially cleared of all charges except for one count of carrying an unlicensed firearm, in a later civil trial one of his victims, who had been left paralyzed and brain damaged by the shooting, won a $43 million settlement against Goetz. [14]

An NAIS overview of the 1980s can be found in the pages of the spring 2006 issue of *Independent School* magazine, a retrospective of the magazine's history. Here are some excerpts:

Rather than any scheme to divert tax money to private education, what turned out to be the most far-reaching event of the 1980s was the publication of "A Nation at

Risk: An Imperative for Educational Reform," which, through its deep criticism of U.S. public education and call to action, set off a flurry of reform efforts that are still felt today. Indeed, the whole standards movement today is essentially a spin-off of that single report.

The magazine editor at the time, Blair McElroy, thought "A Nation at Risk" so significant, she dedicated an entire issue to the topic and reprinted the 12-page "Open Letter to the American Public" section of the report.

Equally significant was NAIS's own report (with the National Association of Secondary School Principals), "A Study of High Schools," which led to the publication of Ted Sizer's *Horace's Compromise*, as well as *The Shopping Mall High School* by Arthur Powell and *American High Schools Since 1940* by Robert Hempel. In the magazine, Sizer outlined his eight principles of essential schools, with particular focus on the "critical triangle of student, teacher, and subject, and the climate in school in which the triangle functions." These would eventually be the guiding principles of the essential schools movement.

Yet, while keeping one eye on the national educational issues, *Independent School* also paid a great deal of attention to life within schools. As one former teacher put it, "Students are wearing shoes again, the faculty room arguments about relevance have subsided, trendy micro-courses are gone from the catalogues, [and] student protest has become an essay topic in the final exam on U.S. History." Meanwhile, the magazine was chock full of articles on gender education, diversity, professional development, trusteeship, moral education, service learning, global education, and, of course, technology—the last of which makes for some of the more humorous writing simply because we have moved so far since then. Consider the question posed in one article: "Will word processing make a difference in the way children write?" Or the article that debated the relative values of PASCEL and BASIC language for teachers when writing their own programs. Or even the careful delineation between "computer literacy" and "computer-assisted learning," and why both are important.

Some of the strongest writing focused on the moral issues in education. In this decade, the magazine would publish Peggy McIntosh's ground-breaking essay, "White Privilege: Unpacking the Invisible Knapsack," and also run a long interview with McIntosh that focused in part on the connection between women's issues and diversity. In the interview, McIntosh criticizes schools for their hierarchical views: "Most schools convey to their students a Darwinian proposition that life is a matter of survival of the fittest and that of necessity, it contains many hierarchies in which only a few people reach the 'top.' School makes people able to see what the 'top' is and urges them to go for it."[15]

In 1965, Intel co-founder Gordon Moore postulated what came to be known as Moore's Law: namely, that computer processing power would double every two years. By the mid-1980s, it was clear that this rapid rate of technological change would accelerate the association toward its adolescent years. Whereas in 1977 Hinrichs requested funds from the Board of Trustees to purchase a new typewriter and a simple copier, consider some of these new technologies that NYSAIS and its member schools adopted in the 1980s, innovations that promised to save both time and resources (while also necessitating time-sucking learning curves that would exasperate the most dedicated educators):

- Take, for example, the changes in storage of computer data. Harken back to the 8-inch floppy disk that stored one to two megabytes of data; the 5.25-inch floppy that stored less than a megabyte; the 3.5-inch diskette that stored over two megabytes; and hard drives the size of a Whitman Sampler box of chocolates that could actually store twenty-five megabytes—an amount equal to a large number of floppies. I can remember, as an assistant head at East Woods School, asking Headmaster Jim Adams if I could invest $999 in one of those zippy new twenty-five megabyte hard drives that would save so much time and hassle. Nowadays, we can pick up a $6.95 thumb drive with eight gigabytes of storage—that's 8,000 megabytes![16]

- Barbara Swanson, who was hired as a part-time associate in 1984, remembers attending a Business Affairs Council meeting at Friends Seminary, when the talk turned to a newfangled contraption. "Someone said, 'Does anybody here have a fax machine?' A few people did. And this person asked them, 'Well, what do you use it for? I can't figure it out. The board thinks we should have one, but I don't know why we need one.'"[17]

- I distinctly remember going to a technology exhibition at the Javits Center in the late 1980s and watching a demonstration of a fancy device that would take the place of the omnipresent and noisy dot-matrix printer. This new laser printer could

NYSAIS

produce documents that looked like pages from a typeset novel. Imagine. I thought I was seeing magic before my eyes.

• From the minutes of the January 23, 1985 Board of Trustees meeting: "Mr. Hinrichs was absent due to inclement weather on the tundra and participated in the meeting [on] the Membership Committee report thanks to the wonders of a speakerphone."

• NYSAIS Associate Director Lois Bailey said, "Visiting committee chairs would probably go home after a school visit with a briefcase full of handwritten sub-reports, and then, using a typewriter, craft those sub-reports into a visiting committee report. I know our chairs are much busier now, but, if you can, imagine the enormity of the task. It sounds like 1842! Gradually, we got into computers, which made the job more and more streamlined. I think the quality probably went up because there wasn't pressure on one person to craft the whole document."[18]

• Swanson vividly remembered learning about a new program that would soon become known as email. "It was pitched at a meeting of state and regional associations at an NAIS-sponsored conference. But it wasn't called email yet. [It was so new] there was no name for this. NAIS wanted to start a pilot project with Apple to teach schools how to use the program, and they wanted one other association. And so we all had to submit proposals of why we should be the ones picked. You also had to have a commitment from ten schools to help pilot this program. So at that same BAC meeting where we talked about fax machines, I said, "And by the way, there's this other thing I want to try. Can I get ten of you to pledge that you will be on board and be part of this pilot?" I had them right there in the room, and they signed up. I submitted the proposal, and we got chosen to do that pilot. And Lois and I went out to Cupertino, California, to be trained in this."[19]

But even as technology was coming to play an increasingly important role in the life of the association, many people looked to NYSAIS and its executive director for more human qualities, namely counseling and advice. As Hinrichs reported to the trustees in June 1982:

> For reasons of economy of time and cash I have always used my personal phone line to conduct NYSAIS's business. This means that the phone is listed in my name only. This saves the expense of a business line, and it also cuts down on the number of calls I get from parents seeking to use the association for educational counseling and from unemployed teachers who think this is a placement agency. Both kinds of calls take a lot of time because they come from people in distress who need someone to listen and sympathize. Even though one gently explains that NYSAIS is not structured to do a proper job of placement, particularly of someone we don't know, it is hard to turn away someone who needs help.[20]

Giving thoughtful advice and counseling to parents, school trustees, teachers, and especially heads of school has always been an important part of the executive director's job—and one that lends an endearing quality to a large organization. This also helps to explain what may be the greatest frustration of executive directors: getting out from under the necessary administration of the association and visiting member schools to see and hear the people the association holds most dear and wants passionately to serve.

The State Board of Regents made its position clear regarding NYSAIS's authority on February 25, 1984 when it stated, "Authority to evaluate and accredit schools in the State of New York is conferred by charter from the Regents of the University of New York. The Regents have chartered NYSAIS to evaluate and accredit elementary and secondary schools in the State of New York."

This was later confirmed by the association, when the board subsequently resolved on June 16, 1986, "The Trustees of NYSAIS reaffirm the resolution endorsed at the Annual Meeting on November 7, 1985, viz, 'The Trustees of the New York State Association of Independent Schools resolve and affirm that accredited schools, having already demonstrated their worth through an evaluation process authorized by the Regents, are free to continue without further justification the educational and testing programs they have developed.'"

Trustee Clem continued to support strengthening the Professional Development Committee, something he would do throughout his association with NYSAIS. That commitment was echoed in the executive director's report from 1984: "Our schools employ more than 5,000 teachers and administrators. For many of them opportunities for professional development are limited by geography and budget. We need to reach them." That same year, to help address these needs and to alleviate the ever-increasing demands of the executive director's job, Hinrichs announced to the board that he had hired Barbara Swanson as a new part-time associate beginning on September 1.[21]

Less than one year into the job, Swanson's presence was already making a substantial difference in professional development opportunities. In addition to trustee education workshops and the annual meeting of the Business Affairs Committee, during the spring of 1985 NYSAIS sponsored teacher workshops on a variety of topics, including "Problem-Solving Using Manipulatives," "Writing Across the Disciplines: A Process Approach," "*Horace's Compromise*," and "Language and Cognition." A total of 202 teachers from seventy-four schools took part in the workshops. Throughout the state, trustee workshops and teacher institutes were coordinated with both the Connecticut Association of Independent Schools and the Independent School Association of Massachusetts. The following year would bring the launch of an Experienced Teacher Workshop on April 19, 1986, further improving the range and reach of the association's professional development services.

In his 1984-85 Report of the Executive Director to the Trustees, Hinrichs observed that over the years "the State, and to some extent, the media and the public, have come to regard NYSAIS as the voice of independent education in New York. It will be important to maintain this regard because it directly affects the kind of attention one commands in official circles as well as attitudes toward independent education generally." Hinrichs added that this was "another year of preoccupation with Albany and the regulations implementing the Regents' Action Plan."[22] Clearly, much of the executive director's time and energy was devoted to keeping a watchful eye on the State, a job that too often member schools could not fully appreciate, busy as they were with keeping their schools running smoothly in spite of an intrusive, politically motivated state bureaucracy.

It was with considerable regret that, at the April 17, 1985 meeting, the board accepted Hinrich's resignation, effective

June 1986. As reported in the board minutes, "the trustees asked the President to establish a search committee and work with Mr. Hinrichs to develop a plan for an orderly transition in the professional leadership of the association. A general depression ensued." The board's respect and appreciation for Hinrichs was surely mutual. When Hinrichs presented his final Report of the Executive Director to the Trustees in June 1986, he closed it by saying, "I concluded my first report with the observation, 'I find that I have a vast amount left to learn. In that sense the job is like the ocean, and perhaps that is why I like it.' For nine years it was a very good job, and I did indeed like it. But there is still a vast amount left to learn, and much of it lies outside the realm of NYSAIS, and that's why I want to move on. What made the job so good was the people I worked with, most particularly you, the Trustees. I am grateful for the understanding and the support you accorded me. I could not have wanted more." [23]

One of the tasks that awaited Hinrich's successor would be managing the growing number of school evaluations. At the April 16, 1986 board meeting, it was reported that 160 evaluators were conducting a total of fifteen ten-year evaluations and ten five-year evaluations. While the evaluators used the *New England Manual*, it was agreed that it was only a matter of time before the association would adopt its own manual, which would incorporate evaluation instructions and the NYSAIS Standards for Membership (which were currently a stand-alone assessment and tended to be treated as an afterthought, rather than as an integral part of the evaluation). It was also agreed that accreditations would become an exclusive function of the association, thus eliminating the use of the Middle States Association accreditation. This would be a critical goal for Hinrichs' successor: Frederick Calder, the longtime headmaster of Ger-

THE NEW YORK STATE ASSOCIATION OF INDEPENDENT SCHOOLS

287 PAWLING AVENUE, TROY, NEW YORK 12180-5238   518-274-0184   FAX 518-274-0185

FREDERICK C. CALDER   *EXECUTIVE DIRECTOR*

N
Y
S
A
I
S

Letterhead, April 1987

mantown Friends School, who was appointed executive director to begin July 1986.[23]

As part of Calder's first 1986-87 Report of the Executive Director to the Trustees, he announced at the April 16, 1987 board meeting that the association's new office would be located at 287 Pawling Avenue, Troy, New York 12180, on the campus of the Emma Willard School, at an annual cost of $1,500.

This proximity to the Capitol offices made it easier to keep an eye on legislation and facilitated more direct lobbying. The new location also made it easier for the executive director to visit more member schools.

Along with establishing a new office and location, dealing with the State Education Department, designing accreditation manuals, counseling constituents, and visiting schools, Calder's plate was piled high with other issues, including:

- Overseeing association publications, including the *Bulletin*, which served as both a fact sheet and a forum for personal observations and opinion; a directory of member schools; and revised versions of the NYSAIS *Profile* and *Choosing a School*.

◇◇◇

What we seek always is the liberty, not
the license, to do with our schools, in
the service of the families we serve,
what we think best, subject to evaluation
by responsible peers and open to the
wisdom of the rest of the educational
community. In that way only can we
preserve and protect for all our schools
and colleges the right to be different.

—Fred Calder, third NYSAIS executive director

◇◇◇

- Preserving the association's fundamental mission,
  namely minding the State and protecting the "independence" of NYSAIS. These goals would prove
  to be Calder's raison d'être right from the beginning of his tenure as executive director. In one of
  his first issues of the *Bulletin*, he wrote, "One of
  my first assignments for NYSAIS was to testify at
  the Annual Legislative Conference of the Board of
  Regents on September 5, 1986 in Albany. It was an
  opportunity once more to think through our mission as schools and to reassert, as we must continu-
  ally do, what we believe and why we exist." He told
  those assembled, "We come to this conference this
  year with no special agenda, no list of monetary or
  other needs. What we seek always is the liberty, not
  the license, to do with our schools, in the service of

the families we serve, what we think best, subject to evaluation by responsible peers and open to the wisdom of the rest of the educational community. In that way only can we preserve and protect for all our schools and colleges the right to be different." [24]

- Organizing the annual conference. The 1986 conference featured "cracker barrel" discussions, general sessions, and a spouse's round table. Topics included "The New Tax Law: Its Impact on Independent Schools," "The Curricular Agenda in the Twentieth Century," "Outside Counseling Services: Controversy or Consensus," and "Strategic Planning for Schools and Colleges."

- Managing relations with the Business Affairs Council. In a letter to the council, Calder outlined how the BAC—one of the oldest committees of the association—fit into the overall structure of NYSAIS: "First, the Trustees reaffirmed the central role of the BAC as providing professional development and support for business officers in our state association. There was clear acknowledgement in our discussions that the complexity of the business officers' jobs in the 1980s, engendered by the explosive growth of government regulation, financial markets, judicial interventions and ruthless commercial practices, no longer compares to the relative simplicity of earlier times. . . . It should be noted, however, that business officers are at present the only group of administrators other than heads that are specifically recognized in the structure of NYSAIS, namely through the BAC and the annual spring conference." [25]

Nearing the end of his first year as executive director, Calder reported on the association's activities at the June 17, 1987 board meeting. In a format similar to his predecessor, he reported on evaluation and accreditation, legislation, regulation, professional development, membership, legal advice, publications, school visits, counseling, and priorities for the next year. Notable items included:

- "NYSAIS monitored literally hundreds of legislative bills, the most pressing of which were reported in the *Bulletin*. Several were of major concern, e.g., a bill limiting schools' property tax exemption, one requiring licensure of teachers, and another threatening the existence of single-sex schools."
- "We produced eight *Bulletins* and several special letters during 1986-87 as a way of keeping the membership informed. The *Bulletin* goes to some 500 readers and we try to keep it intelligible and not too dull. Also, the *Directory*, a *Profile*, and *Choosing a School* are ongoing publications. Information and opinion (helpful, we hope) have been steadily provided to our member schools through hundreds of phone calls. NYSAIS is clearly a telephone business."
- "The Professional Development Committee is a strength."[26]

Other major issues from Calder's first years include:
- Addressing the high dropout rate among accreditation committee members, a daunting administrative task, especially given the amount of time and effort devoted to the initial planning of these committees. At the same time, Calder expressed his

gratitude to those heads and teachers who took time away from their own schools to do such valuable work for the association and independent school education.

- Changing the NYSAIS fiscal year from August 31 to June 30, as reported in the minutes of the June 16-17, 1987 trustee meeting, pending notification of the IRS.

- Expanding BAC's functions. In 1987-88, BAC assumed responsibility for a major component of NYSAIS's administrative services. Bylaws were drafted and subsequently

Executive Director Fred Calder

approved by the Board of Trustees: "With careful guidance and judicious use of time, the BAC should in future contribute markedly to strengthening the management of our schools."[27]

- Strengthening membership regulations for the Athletic Association. "After considerable deliberation on the continuing problem of non-NYSAIS members joining the NYSAIS Athletic Association, trustees voted that all members of the Athletic Association must be members of NYSAIS effective July 1, 1990."[28]

- Launching the first conference for assistant school heads. At the end of the decade, a group of assistant heads of school in New York met with Swanson to form a committee that assembled a program for the first NYSAIS Conference for Assistant Heads. Having served on that committee, I had the opportunity to see how she motivated and inspired member schools to think big and facilitate better professional development for all groups. In a short period of time, this conference evolved into what is now the Division Heads Annual Conference, which is held each year at Mohonk.

As alluded to earlier in my interview with Tom Hogan, probably one of the decade's more momentous developments for independent schools was the formation of the New York State Coalition for Nonpublic Education, which NYSAIS greeted with enthusiasm. The coalition consisted of six major private school groups: Agudath Israel of America, the Association of Christian Schools International, the Board of Jewish Education of Greater New York, the Lutheran Schools Association, the New York State Council of Catholic School Superintendents, and NYSAIS. Together, they comprised more than 90 percent of all private schools in New York state. "The major purpose of the coalition was to combine forces," Hogan explained, "either for promoting the interests of private education or defending it against onslaughts from any quarter. This coalition gave NYSAIS added strength in its dealings with the state government and its agencies."

Yet issues of personal character also continued to loom large for the association. Writing about his priorities for 1989-90, Calder stated, "We must continue our sometimes lonely advocacy of ethical behavior both among and within our schools. There is no avoiding the fact that our constituents look more and more to our schools as the transmitters of moral standards." Ongoing issues included hiring and firing, admissions practices, boards and heads, tax laws, and "how we speak about schools other than our own."[29]

The close of the decade found the trustees and the executive director establishing the following goals for the 1990s:

1. The evaluation and accreditation process: developing and strengthening the trustee evaluation section and training new visiting committee chairs and assistant chairs.

2. Developing NYSAIS Athletic Association regulations and clarifying the issue of postseason play, including possible new policies.

3. Maintaining an intensive school-visiting program by the executive director.

4. Strengthening ties with other nonpublic schools through the New York State Coalition for Nonpublic Education.

5. Monitoring state government, including lobbying work and maintaining contact with the State Education Department.

6. Strengthening institutional counseling, including legal research as provided by the NYSAIS central office.

YOUTH CULTURE VIA MUSIC

To better understand youth culture of the 1990s we only have to look—and listen—more closely to their music. Here's a sampling of *Billboard* magazine's top pop songs and artists from the decade, and the number of weeks each hit spent at the top of the charts:

1990 "Vision of Love" by Mariah Carey (4)
1991 "Black or White" by Michael Jackson (7)
1992 "I Will Always Love You" by Whitney Houston (14)
1993 "That's the Way Love Goes" by Janet Jackson (8)
1994 "I'll Make Love to You" by Boyz II Men (14)
1995 "One Sweet Day" by Mariah Carey & Boyz II Men (16)
1996 "Macarena" by Los Del Rio (Bayside Boys Mix) (14)
1997 "Candle in the Wind" by Elton John (14)
1998 "The Boy Is Mine" by Brandy & Monica (13)
1999 "Smooth" by Santana (12)[1]

CHAPTER FIVE

Adolescent Years: 1990s

Ah, to be an adolescent again! Ah, no, thank you! So many confusing life experiences confront adolescents as high school begins—adventures to grab hold of, or let go of. Boys' development finally starts catching up with girls'. Cliques, social circles, and romances—perceived or otherwise—abound. So do questions: Who am I, anyway? I need to assess where I'm going, what I want out of life, and stand on my own. What to eat, drink, and smoke? Adolescents push back against parental control as a matter of principle, all the while wondering, "How the hell am I going to get out of this situation and convince mom and dad I am capable of driving a car?" First jobs where the money earned stays in one's pocket. Should I go to college? Why do I need to go when I can backpack in Europe—and I won't have to take those dreadful SATs? Music choices: The Beatles? Alternative rock? Grunge music? Gangsta rap? Hip-hop? Pop? Classical? All of the above? None of the above?

During its own adolescent years, NYSAIS was pondering

some of the same kinds of questions, but in a slightly different form. Why wouldn't the State and its Board of Regents just let go? We weren't candles in the wind. We could, and would, stand on our own. Other nonpublic schools that were once independent of each other were now banding together to battle the mighty state bureaucracy. Financial sustainability was growing, thanks to all the professional development activity and services offered to NYSAIS's growing numbers of members. The well-being of those members was nurtured through the steady and sustained counseling NYSAIS provided to heads, trustees, parents, and teachers. The evaluation process had now taken on a life of its own. With the manual and tools available at this point, how could a two-person office find the volunteers to do the necessary work to evaluate all the schools seeking accreditation? And could the association's leader visit with all the member schools in a year?

Our lives are shaped by the events around us. That's especially true during adolescence, when it is difficult enough to navigate the treacherous waters of the teen years, without also being swamped by external events that push and pull at our self-image. Those events constantly force us to ask, "Who am I, and where do I fit into this life?" Such was the case for our association.

When we look at a small sample of the events of the 1990s through a world lens, we see:

1990 Nelson Mandela freed from prison; Hubble telescope launched into space; Lech Walesa becomes first democratically elected president of Poland.

1991 The Soviet Union collapses; Operation Desert Storm is launched after Iraq invades Kuwait; South Africa repeals apartheid laws.

1992 The Cold War officially comes to an end; riots in Los Angeles follow the acquittal of four white police officers in the beating of Rodney King.

1993 Terrorists detonate a truck bomb in the North Tower of the World Trade Center; federal and state marshals raid the Branch Davidian compound in Waco, Texas; use of the Internet grows exponentially.

1994 800,000 Tutsis perish in the Rwandan Genocide; Channel Tunnel opens, connecting Britain and France; Nelson Mandela elected president of South Africa; O. J. Simpson arrested for double murder.

1995 Religious cult stages sarin gas attack in Tokyo subway; domestic terrorists bomb the Oklahoma City federal building; Yitzhak Rabin is assassinated.

1996 The Unabomber is arrested; Prince Charles and Princess Diana divorce.

1997 The Hale-Bopp Comet becomes visible from earth; Tiger Woods wins the Masters; Scientists clone sheep; Princess Diana dies in a car crash.

1998 India and Pakistan test nuclear weapons; *Titanic* becomes the most successful movie of all time; Viagra is released on the market; U.S. President Clinton is impeached.

1999 Two students carry out a mass shooting at Columbine High School; the Euro becomes the new European currency; JFK, Jr. dies in a plane accident; Y2K bug threatens to wreak havoc with computers; control of the Panama Canal is returned to Panama.[2]

When we look at the events of the 1990s through an NAIS *Independent School* magazine lens, we see:

1990 Peggy McIntosh's "White Privilege: Unpacking the Invisible Knapsack" appears. It becomes the magazine's most requested reprint.

1991 John Esty, Jr. retires as president of NAIS. Catherine O'Neill takes over the reins as magazine editor and NAIS's director of publications; Peter Relic's first column as NAIS president is published.

1992 A package of stories on the teaching of math and science; Pearl Rock Kane interviews Robert Coles. Sexuality education in the age of AIDS.

1993 NAIS relocates to Washington, D.C. Articles on experiential education—and a report from Washington by Kiki Johnson, then a policy analyst in the U.S. Department of Education. A look at trusteeship in an eight-article package.

1994 Time for redesign! The magazine unveils its new look, and NAIS unveils its new logo. A survey of international education programs. A new department, "Independent School Parent," debuts with an essay by Dr. Ned Hallowell.

1995 What lower schools have to teach their elders. A cover story on fundraising, with guidance from Helen Colson about organizing the development office. An issue devoted almost entirely to environmental education.

1996 A prescient review by Steve Clem calls independent educators' attention to Daniel Goleman's work on emotional intelligence; Bob Riddle of Crossroads School calls on independent educators to address gay and lesbian issues. A package of features on teaching in the '90s—with nary a mention of technology. An issue on athletics at independent schools.

1997 The arts in education—and the first 100-plus-page issue. "Summer School," a poem by future Poet Laureate Billy Collins. Editor Michael Brosnan's first issue focuses on children's peer relationships, and features a cover story by Michael G. Thompson.

1998 Feature on the changing independent school family. Aspects of headship—and a cluster of articles on charter schools.

1999 Equity and justice—and an excerpt from Michael Thompson and Daniel Kindlon's best-selling *Raising Cain: Understanding the Emotional Lives of Boys*. The "M Word" moves into the forefront with an article on marketing your school. The teaching life, and Nancy and Ted Sizer on moral education.[3]

Using a NYSAIS lens, we can drill down even further and see the issues the association grappled with throughout the decade. To do this, we only have to look at the *NYSAIS Bulletin* and the topics Executive Director Fred Calder chose to write about:

1990 "Teaching Toward Destitution" (#145), "Contracts Pure and Simple" (#148)

1991 "What Do Parents Want?" (#157), "The Joys and Sorrows of Choice" (#158)

1992 "The Persistence of Private Schools" (#167), "The Conundrum of Diversity" (#156)

1993 "The Disappearance of Content" (#175), "Choice and the First Amendment" (#176), "The Technology Revolution in Learning" (#184)

1994 "Three Perspectives on Strategic Planning" (#185), "Why Tuition Remission" (#186), "To Be an Adult" (#193)

1995 "The Politics of Education" (#195), "The Perils of Responsibility" (#197), "Respecting Trustees" (#198), "The Morality of Compensation" (#202), "Concepts Without Content" (#204)

1996 "School Report Cards" (#208), "Deconstructing Education" (#212), "Tyranny of the Minority" (#214)

1997 "Taking the Fifth" (#215), "Vive La Difference" (#216)

1998 "Central Planning Versus Local Initiative" (#128), "The Virtue of Failure" (#228), "The Primacy of Mission" (#232)

1999 "The Fundraising Imperative" (#236), "Sustainability" (#237), "Getting to No" (#241), "Testing as Education" (#242)[4]

As we make our way through this decade, we will see that with strong leadership—at the board and staff levels—dedicated, hard-working people forged an association that not only survived, but thrived as it approached adulthood in a new century. This vitality was evident in the association's numerous publications, including an ever-expanding membership directory; the *NYSAIS Bulletin*; *BAC Talk*, the Business Affairs Council's regularly published newsletter; the Accreditation and Evaluation Manual; and a fledgling, user-friendly website.

The annual *NYSAIS Membership Directory* is a perfect

illustration of how the association developed throughout the 1990s. Published in 1990, the fourth edition ran twenty-two pages, with member schools listed by district (e.g., Western Lakes, Hudson Valley, New York City, and Long Island) with their basic information.

1990 NYSAIS Directory cover

By 1999, the *Membership Directory* had grown to thirty-six pages, and included a compendium of association information:

- Profile [Mission]
- NYSAIS Offices information
- NYSAIS Board of Trustees
- Member Schools listed by district and out of country
- Association Members [affiliated programs such as Prep for Prep]
- Athletic Association
- Alphabetical Listing
- Professional Development Programs
    o The Effective Board of Trustees
    o Beginning Teachers Institute
    o NYSAIS/CAIS Annual Conference
    o Information Technology Specialists Conference
    o Assistant Heads/Division Heads Conference
    o Experienced Teachers Institute

- o Athletic Directors Conference
- o NYSAIS/CAIS Business Affairs Conference
- Non-Discriminatory Statement

The association opened the 1990s with 140 member schools, serving some 50,000 students in nursery, elementary, and secondary schools. The board established various membership levels, including regular, provisional, correspondent, association, honorary, and athletic.[5] Seventy-seven of those member schools were accredited by NYSAIS. In his Executive Director's 1990 Annual Report, Calder provided the board with some useful context about how independent schools fit into the bigger picture: "In New York State alone," he wrote, "there are some 2,200 private schools, nearly all of them religiously based. NYSAIS comprises about 6.5 percent of the total number of schools, though nearer 12 percent of the total number of students."[6]

Meanwhile, the Athletic Executive Committee sought to help its member schools find their footing, whether as members of the New York State Public High School Athletic Association or by beginning to assert their independence and developing their own regulations. Increasingly, athletic directors of member schools would be asked to undertake this important mission.[6]

In 1990, participation at conferences, workshops, and other meetings jumped to 1,658, an increase of over 300 from the previous year's numbers. In addition to sponsoring these sessions, the year would see the formation of a New Heads Support Group and the publication of eight *NYSAIS Bulletins*, *A Legal Primer for Trustees of the New York Independent Schools*, and occasional letters and announcements. Much professional development work continued to focus on multicultural education, gender issues, global affairs, and different learning styles. And the following year, the Fourth Annual NAIS Conference for People of Color at Independent Schools was held in New York City, December 12–14, 1991.

In his 1990-91 Annual Executive Director's Report, Calder drew attention to the evaluation and accreditation process:

> At a time when conditions in the marketplace are forc-
> ing closer and closer scrutiny of all private schools,
> accreditation becomes an even more important desig-
> nation and confers simultaneously a heavier responsibil-
> ity on the accrediting body. Literally hundreds of people
> from the Commission on Accreditation to the evaluators
> themselves labor each year to make the process rigor-
> ous, honest, and ultimately credible. As the independent
> school in America struggles to stay competitive, there
> is no doubt that regular evaluation of all aspects of the
> institution will be a major factor in the mathematics of
> survival.[7]

In the February 1991 *Bulletin*, Calder demonstrated his prescience when he observed, "Virtually everyone seems to have read, or read about John Chubb and Terry Moe's *Politics, Markets and America's Schools*. Private school people are thrilled at last to have an 'objective' study, from the Brookings Institute no less, that proclaims their superiority. Public-school people are less thrilled, if not to say enraged." (Two decades later, John Chubb would become president of NAIS.)[8]

Peter D. Relic, then the new president of NAIS, began his tenure in Boston the same time I began mine as a head of school in Connecticut, on July 1, 1991. It was my good fortune that Peter and I both attended NAIS's annual weeklong summer orientation program for new heads of school, held at the Dana Hall School in Wellesley, Massachusetts. In one of the first papers he wrote as president, entitled "School Choice ≠ Politics; School Choice = Justice," Relic posited:

> No child should be locked into a school which fails to educate. If the school cannot or will not change, parents should be able to seek an alternative, which works well. Court after court has ruled that the quality of education must not be a function of the wealth of the family or of the school district. Finally, through choice, we will have the means to create a solution, based on the principles of equal access and justice.[9]

The American educational community was then steeped in a debate over whether to direct tax dollars to provide support for alternative education beyond public schooling, including vouchers, state subsidies, and tax credits. This issue would consume much time throughout the decade, not only for NYSAIS but also for other state and regional associations. The NYSAIS Board of Trustees and executive director published a "Statement on Aspects of Educational Choice" in June 1991.[10]

The 1990s witnessed another movement in education: a shift from strict, cognitive-based goals and objectives toward noncognitive-based elements of child development, such as character and values. This trend was mirrored in some of the related popular books of the decade, including Martin Seligman's *Learned Optimism* (Vintage, 1990), William Bennett's *The Book of Virtues* (Simon & Schuster, 1993), and Daniel Goleman's *Emotional Intelligence: Why It Can Matter More Than IQ* (Bantam, 1995).

A similar evolution was taking place within the association.

Throughout the 1990s, the "Profile" section of the membership directory stated, "Established originally to protect independent schools from obstructive legislation and regulation, NYSAIS has added substantially to the range of its activities since its founding. These activities include:

- Evaluation and accreditation of member schools
- Professional development for faculty, administrators, and trustees
- Advocacy for independent education
- Legal and institutional counsel
- Information on legislation, regulations, statistics, educational developments, and administrative practice."

Increasingly, the board and executive director were moving beyond basic services to a more personalized approach to supporting member schools. Good examples were the establishment of "Principles of Good Practice," which helped schools build trust through delineating hiring practices, responsible trusteeship, enrollment contracts, and conflict-of-interest policies, and the finely tuned "Trustee Policy Statement on NYSAIS Advisory Services." In part, this policy stated that when "NYSAIS is called upon to aid a school in crisis, the consent of all parties is required. NYSAIS works for its member school, not for individual persons or groups within it. To help strengthen the headship and general governance of our schools, and to try to anticipate crisis instead of succumbing to it, NYSAIS offers the following services:

1. New Heads Support Program
2. The Executive Director of NYSAIS is available for consultation and workshops
3. Consultant Advisory Service, where the executive

director will pair schools needing support with appropriate consultants

4. The Business Affairs Council can provide assistance to member schools

5. Consultative Committee of Trustees and Heads to assist in matters of governance, issues of communications, problem solving, and evaluations."[11]

Clearly, Calder saw that the sustainability of the association and its member schools required going beyond basic oversight services and providing a nurturing outreach approach to education and the care of schools, families, faculties, and, most importantly, children. And yet, NYSAIS could not forget these basic services any more than independent school parents could forget homework, testing, and college placements. As part of "basic services," Calder reported in his 1992-93 Annual Report:

- . . . the variance application process (a thing of beauty, as government procedures go) that NYSAIS negotiated with [State Education] Commissioner Ambach in 1986 was essentially scrapped. In its place the SED [State Education Department] imposed the new Nonpublic School Variance procedure to which all private schools must adhere. Though several concessions were granted to distinguish the new procedure from the public school version, it is nevertheless, much more tortuous and much less 'user friendly' than its predecessor. As with all such complicating changes that seek greater compliance with government regulations, the result may be exactly the opposite.

As denizens of the "information age," we see a deplorable tendency to bury everyone in paper, faxes, e-mail and general undisciplined verbiage. One of NYSAIS' greatest challenges is to provide its member schools with information they need while not succumbing to the widely held belief that more is better.

—Fred Calder, third NYSAIS executive director

- In this school year 1,830 people participated in professional development programs.
- As of this writing some 112 schools are either already accredited by NYSAIS or are scheduled for their first evaluation during the next several years.
- Total association membership changed little.
- The mysteries and delights of interscholastic athletics continued to challenge those charged with their execution.
- The quality of independent school governance was once again a foremost concern of the association. Recognizing that the effectiveness of lay trustees will be crucial to the survival of private education and that communication between heads and trustees is the sine qua non of good governance, NYSAIS Trustees amended the bylaws to allow school trustees to serve on the NYSAIS Board.
- Once again the NYSAIS Business Affairs Council consisting of 16 business officers from member

schools gave prodigiously of their time and talent to strengthen independent education.

- As denizens of the 'information age,' we see a deplorable tendency to bury everyone in paper, faxes, e-mail and general undisciplined verbiage. One of NYSAIS' greatest challenges is to provide its member schools with information they need while not succumbing to the widely held belief that more is better.[12]

In 1993, in what immediately became a tradition, CAIS heads were invited to attend the annual NYSAIS conference. As the new head of a Connecticut school (and one who had come from a NYSAIS school), this was a welcome development for me and for all Connecticut school heads, especially since CAIS's membership was just half of NYSAIS's. How we all looked forward to joining our New York colleagues each November at Mohonk Mountain House. I particularly appreciated this special independent school union because I eventually became the president of the CAIS Board of Trustees. This same year saw another first, when "lay trustees" were invited to sit on the NYSAIS board. As a welcome letter to the new board members explained, "The primary reason for the change is that issues of governance and management have become more and more crucial to our schools' survival and health, and that the partnership between heads and boards needs all the support we can give it."

By now, the association's reserves had grown to such an extent that the board tasked the Investment Committee to formulate an investment policy. (The board's confidence in the Investment Committee was evident in minutes of the June 9, 1994 board meeting: "The committee was commended for its fog-dispersing lucidity of thought and expression.") Later that month, in a letter to the association's heads of school, Calder and Board Chair Edes Gilbert of the Spence School asked all member schools to adopt and install CONNECT, INC. software that would network schools for email and electronic files.

To improve its long-term planning, the association conducted its own strategic planning process in 1994. Highlights from the "Strategic Planning Committee Report to the NYSAIS Board of Trustees" included:

- The committee recommended that one associate director have primary responsibility for administering evaluations.
- In comparison to the Middle States Association of Colleges and Schools, NYSAIS evaluation fees were extremely modest, generating approximately $25,000 per year and meeting perhaps half of the cost of the program. The committee recommended doubling evaluation fees over a two-year period.
- To relieve pressure on full-time personnel, the committee recommended hiring part-time professionals to perform certain functions.
- With the reserve fund totaling about $290,000, the committee recommended that the board consider a more aggressive management of the funds, similar to a school endowment, with the goal of producing annual revenue for the operating budget and long-term growth that slightly exceeded inflation.[13]

In his 1994-95 Annual Report, Calder wrote about the implications of the end of Mario Cuomo's twelve-year tenure as governor and the election of George Pataki. The new governor had already called for drastic cuts in the State Education Department, which prompted Calder to state, "On the other

The truth is that if all NYSAIS schools actually spent the NAIS recommended 1 percent of their budgets on professional growth, these numbers [1,681 attendees at 35 events] would double or triple. And though the burden for NYSAIS under such circumstances would be daunting, it is a challenge that we would gladly accept.

—Fred Calder, third NYSAIS executive director

hand, the bureaucracy in its confusion and anxiety sought the refuge of inaction, and though routine business bumped along, important initiatives were quietly sidetracked. Such circumstances tend to be welcomed by independent schools since we are generally far more upset by what the state does than by what it does not do." On a more positive note, Calder applauded the many volunteers who continued to chair and serve on visiting accreditation committees. "This year, 130 NYSAIS teachers and administrators gave up four days (and nights) of their professional time on 19 separate committees to complete the rigorous process that candidate schools must undergo." And, in the area of professional development, Calder reported that there were thirty-five events that attracted 1,681 people from member schools and some from out of state. He went on to say, "The truth is that if all NYSAIS schools actually spent the NAIS recommended 1 percent of their budgets on professional growth, these numbers would double or triple. And though the burden for NYSAIS under such circumstances would be daunting, it is a challenge that we would gladly accept."[14]

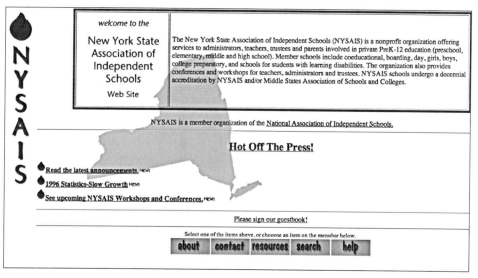

NYSAIS website home page, December 19, 1996

By mid-decade, the reputation of the association and its staff was so strong that it inspired many willing volunteers from member schools. Volunteers served not only on visiting accreditation committees, but also on the Athletic Executive Committee, Business Affairs Committee, Board of Trustee committees (Finance, Executive, Governance, Membership, Nominating), Professional Development Committee, Technology Committee, numerous conference planning committees, and as representatives to NAIS.

It was in 1996 that the association found its way onto the Internet. At a board meeting, "the chairman of the technology committee brought a recommendation for establishment of a NYSAIS worldwide web page. Trustees responded enthusiastically and approved a $4,500.00 appropriation to be matched by E. E. Ford funds. Barbara and Lois will begin negotiations with the provider, Soho Internetwork Company, immediately."[15] A short time thereafter, NYSAIS made its online debut at www.

nysais.org, with a website featuring its mission, programs, and up-to-date membership information. For the first time, the 1996-1997 *NYSAIS Membership Directory* included email and URL website addresses for a small number of member schools.

The camaraderie and sense of unity so common among independent school educators were particularly strong among association directors and NAIS leadership. At the annual conference, NYSAIS and CAIS heads combined forces—as a conference planning committee and in attendance—to expand their ever-growing independent school network and reconnect with one another; at the same time, each also reserved a portion of the three-day event to hold their respective separate annual meetings. In another kind of independent school collaboration, NYSAIS, NAIS, and other state and regional associations rose up and responded in unison to a plan by *U.S. News and World Report* to rank independent secondary schools the same way it did colleges and universities. The answer was an unequivocal "No!" from NYSAIS and NAIS.

In an unprecedented decision, the board approved a "working sabbatical" for Calder, following his eleven years of service to the association. The sabbatical amounted to a busman's holiday: Calder spent one day a week at NYSAIS monitoring state government issues, while also publishing the *NYSAIS Bulletin*, attending NYSAIS events, and being available by phone to discuss important governance matters and other issues with heads or board chairs. He spent the balance of his sabbatical serving as interim director of the Ethical Culture Fieldston School during the 1997-98 academic year. The board noted that "This prospect would, among other things, recharge his batteries and acquaint him intimately with the experience of heading an independent school in the '90s."[16] Ken Barton, former longtime head of school at the Fieldston School, served as deputy executive director in Calder's absence. Another key change was Barbara Swanson's decision to move to Nashville, Tennessee, although she remained committed to her job with NYSAIS, working from her Nashville home and commuting to conferences, institutes, and board meetings.[17]

Nineteen-ninety-seven was a banner year for NYSAIS. Not only did the association celebrate its 50th anniversary, but it did so in robust health. Enrollment in member schools was up by 1.6 percent; the association's fiscal reserves exceeded the cost of a year's operations; and the board extended an invitation to New Jersey heads of school to the next annual conference.[17]

In 1998, the board approved the formation of a Diversity Subcommittee of the Professional Development Committee. This, together with the establishment of the People of Color Job Fair, was an important step in building the association's diversity awareness. Also crucial were NYSAIS's partnerships with outside organizations, including Early Steps, which helped place kindergarten and first grade children of color into New York City independent schools, and Prep for Prep, an NYSAIS member that over its thirty-five-year history placed more than 2,700 students at fifty-two NYSAIS member schools. Aileen Hefferren, chief executive of Prep for Prep, has observed, "Our students thrive at these independent schools, both in and out of the classroom, and then go on to serve as alumni leaders, donors, faculty members, and administrators. Today, twenty-three Prep alums are teachers or administrators at NYSAIS member schools. A dozen are parents of enrolled students, often at their parents' alma maters."[18]

During this same period, NYSAIS rallied with other independent schools in the battle against standardized testing, joining an *amicus curiae* brief in a challenge filed by the Columbus School in Ohio against state testing.[19] In the October 1999

NYSAIS Bulletin, Calder used his eloquent and to-the-point pen to articulate the association's stance on testing:

> The country is fixated on the efficacy of standardized tests. The presidential candidates proclaim them; even New York's Regents seem to have embraced them. The tests, they say, are the answer to abysmal student performance in failed schools. By the design of harder tests and teachers being held accountable, students will be goaded to perform better. And, best of all, politicians can claim victory for improving American education. The voices of those who know something about teaching and learning are stilled by the clamor of popular opinion. Clearly, it is a time to stay calm but firm until this too passes.[20]

As NYSAIS prepared to enter the new millennium—neatly sidestepping Y2K (a.k.a. "The Year 2000 Problem"), when it was feared that coding glitches would bring down computer networks around the globe—it would be useful to step back and take stock:

- NYSAIS now served 152 schools that enrolled some 58,000 students; it was affiliated with NAIS and the New York State Coalition for Nonpublic Education.
- Its financial reserves now totaled $476,000.[21]
- It had further strengthened its support for athletics at member schools when the board adopted the *NYSAIS Guidelines for Interscholastic Athletics*, which included statements on philosophy and guidelines.
- The board approved the following changes regarding accreditation:

o The commission on accreditation would be enlarged from 16 to 20 members;

o The commission would develop its own manual;

o Schools that opted for Middle States accreditation were also required to have a one-day visit by the NYSAIS Commission; and

o New member schools would need to be accredited by NYSAIS.[22]

As the association confidently sauntered from adolescence into adulthood, there is one last lens through which we might view NYSAIS, a lens that has been closely focused on the association over the past 50 years, and from many different perspectives. Dr. Richard (Dick) Barter's independent school career is an illustrious one. A longtime devotee of the association, he served as head of four NYSAIS schools, and as president of the NYSAIS Board of Trustees (1975-77), the NAIS Board of Trustees, and the Ohio Association of Independent Schools. He has this to say about the association's value to education:

I do believe the triumvirate of NYSAIS early leaders [Harry Meislahn, Ap Mason, Steve Hinrichs] provided critical and essential professional services for all schools to grow and improve in many critical and core professional and pedagogical areas. The association has grown from an Albany watchdog service to an ever-increasing and improving, high-quality standard-bearer of the best education available in New York. We are distinctive, and let us always be careful not to slip in the selfserving description "better," and we do provide services and experience often not available, either by design, Board of Regents mandate, or Constitutional prohibition. School choice and quality choice continue to be a very valued and distinctive contribution that the "nonpublic" schools provide for our citizens. It is also important to remember, and to retain, this standard of independence that the leadership of NYSAIS has provided at critical points in our collective evolution. Thus a knowledge of, and understanding of, the issues and accomplishments of the past serve as a useful, if not essential, message for the current standard-bearers who are guiding us ever forward into an increasingly challenging but exciting future. Aren't we fortunate to be so well positioned to serve and guide future generations of professional educators.[23]

CHAPTER SIX

Adult Years: 2000s and Beyond

Now that NYSAIS had become a full-fledged adult, with over fifty years of growth and experience under its belt, not only did it run efficiently on all levels, but it also began to model for other associations what they could do to best support their membership. Having an experienced executive director, staff, and Board of Trustees triggered maximum growth and prosperity. The association provided support to its members in the form of professional conferences, training, accreditation, guidance on athletics, expert advice, and financial and good governance practices. Being an adult association would prove to be more important than ever in this new millennium. Unforeseen events would challenge schools and families like never before, particularly in New York City.

At the close of the 1990s and its own adolescent years, the association—along with educational institutions throughout the United States—was rocked by the April 20, 1999 massacre at Columbine High School in Colorado. In less than an hour, Eric

Harris and Dylan Klebold, both seniors, shot and killed twelve students and one teacher; they also wounded more than twenty other students before taking their own lives.[1] It was then the deadliest high school shooting in U.S. history; tragically, it was far from the last, and it sparked an intense debate on gun violence, mental illness, and school safety that continues to this day. Nevertheless, it was a tribute to the association's growing maturity that it was able to guide and support its member schools, not only through the Columbine tragedy but through even tougher times yet to come.

From this point in our narrative, I have been able to draw not only from Board of Trustee documents, executive director reports, NYSAIS publications, interviews, and Internet resources, but also from my twenty-five years of personal experience with the association. I began my apprenticeship with NYSAIS in the late 1980s while working at East Woods School on Long Island, serving on the Professional Development Committee and as a volunteer staff member with the Beginning Teachers Institute and one of the founders of the Assistant Heads Conference (which eventually became the Division Heads Conference). When I moved on to my first headship at a school in Connecticut in 1991, I learned more about the workings of an independent school state association by serving the Connecticut Association of Independent Schools (CAIS) as a member of its professional development, technology, and accreditation committees; its Board of Trustees executive committee; and eventually as the president of its board. It was through this work, and the support of many mentors and patient colleagues, that I came not only to respect but to love the vibrant culture and structure of independent schools—feelings that were only deepened by my work with NAIS, where I served as chair of the editorial board of *Independent School* magazine, and by the opportunities I've had to write on education, leadership, and nonprofit governance for different publications.

After eleven years in Connecticut, I decided to submit my resignation to my board in March of 2001, effective July 2002. As I began my search for a new school, I was introduced to the world of Montessori education and found myself accepting a headship on December 5, 2001 for Brooklyn Heights Montessori School, which happily led me back to New York, ready and willing to serve NYSAIS again. I have now personally witnessed its growth as head of a member school; chair of the Professional Development Committee; member of the Guild of Independent Schools of New York City Board of Trustees; chair of numerous visiting Accreditation Committees; director of the Beginning Teachers Institute; faculty member with the Experienced Teachers Institute; annual conference planner; chair of the Council on Professional Learning and Collaboration; member of all Think Tank sessions; presenter at various conferences; member of the Executive Director Search Committee; secretary of the Board of Trustees; and now as part-time staff member administering the Experienced Leaders Advising Schools (ELAS) program.

Historical perspectives can be helpful in understanding NYSAIS's growth. Here are some snapshots from Future Timeline.net of what was happening in the world during the 2000s:

2000 The dot-com bubble bursts; Vladimir Putin is elected president of Russia; personal home computers break the 1-GHz barrier; Sydney hosts the Olympic Games.

2001 Wikipedia is launched; George W. Bush is sworn in as the 43rd President of the United States; Space station *Mir* is deorbited; Apple launches the iPod; a devastating terrorist attack leaves 3,000 dead in America.

2002 The controversial No Child Left Behind Act (NCLB) is approved by Congress and signed into law by President Bush on January 8, 2002[2]; the Euro enters circulation; the world's first cyborg is created.

2003 The U.S. invasion of Iraq begins and Iraqi President Saddam Hussein is captured by U.S. troops; the space shuttle *Columbia* is destroyed during re-entry; the Human Genome Project is completed; MySpace is launched; China launches its first manned space mission.

2004 Web 2.0 emerges, allowing users to interact with online content; the first privately funded human spaceflight takes place; Facebook is launched; the world's first 1-gigabyte secure digital (SD) memory card is introduced; George W. Bush is re-elected; the Indian Ocean earthquake and resulting tsunami leave a quarter of a million dead.

2005 YouTube is launched; USB flash drives replace floppy disks; in the latest incarnation of the "Scopes Monkey Trial," the U.S. District Court of Pennsylvania rules in the case of *Kitzmiller v. Dover Area School District* that teaching "intelligent design" as an alternative to evolution is a violation of the First Amendment[2]; suicide bombers in London kill fifty-six people, injure 700 others; Hurricane Katrina devastates New Orleans; Angela Merkel is elected the first female chancellor of Germany.

2006 Crude oil production reaches a plateau; Twitter is launched; North Korea conducts its first nuclear test; Saddam Hussein is executed.

2007 The global economic downturn begins; Apple debuts the iPhone; President Bush authorizes a troop surge to respond to growing instability in Iraq; Amazon releases the Kindle; Benazir Bhutto is assassinated in Pakistan.

2008 Dmitry Medvedev is elected president of Russia; oil prices hit a record high; the Internet continues to boom; scientists extract images directly from the brain.

2009 Barack Obama is sworn in as 44th president of the United States, the first African-American to hold the office; the Great Recession deepens, with unemployment hitting 10 percent in late 2009; scientists map the genetic codes of skin and lung cancer; water is discovered on the moon; the Common Core State Standards Initiative, "a state-led effort coordinated by the National Governors Association Center for Best Practices and the Council of Chief State School Officers," is launched[2]; 3D scanning enters the consumer market; the Burj Khalifa, the tallest man-made structure in history, is completed; Africa's population reaches one billion.[2]

2012 On December 14, Adam Lanza, 20, kills his mother and then invades Sandy Hook Elementary School, where he kills twenty children and six adults, including principal Dawn Hochsprung and psychologist Mary Sherlach, making this the second-deadliest mass shooting by a single person in U.S. history.[2]

In a decade marked by disruption, the defining tragedy for New York and the entire United States occurred on September 11, 2001. I distinctly remember that gorgeous morning, particularly the beautiful blue sky. I was scheduled to travel from my school in Kensington, Connecticut to the Hotchkiss School for a CAIS Board of Trustees meeting, but I began my day the way I usually did: teaching my fifth grade mathematics class. In the middle of that class, a teacher walked in and said that I should turn on the television and witness what was taking place in New York City. There it was for all of us to see, the sight of the Twin Towers being ravaged by two planes. I remember calling the CAIS executive director and canceling our board meeting. Events simply demanded that heads of school remain with their students and faculty to console, reflect, and attempt to understand what had just happened. This process continued in the weeks and months that followed, as can be seen in the NYSAIS website home page from September 24, 2001.

As of June 2000, the NYSAIS letterhead displayed a new address. The move from 287 Pawling Road in Troy to 12 Jay Street in Schenectady—an 18-minute drive—meant the staff continued to enjoy ready access to the state capitol but in more spacious quarters.[3]

In its newly adult years, the association increasingly broadened its focus to include the national arena. At its June 21, 2001 meeting, the board heard a presentation on the Advocacy Initiative, a joint effort to promote independent education, sponsored by a coalition of state and regional associations, under the aegis of NAIS. With "power transferring from Washington to states on educational issues, a shift in attitudes about non-profits, regulatory interference, compliance binds, accountability, standardized testing, negative media portrayals of independent schools, changing demographics, charter and for-profit school,

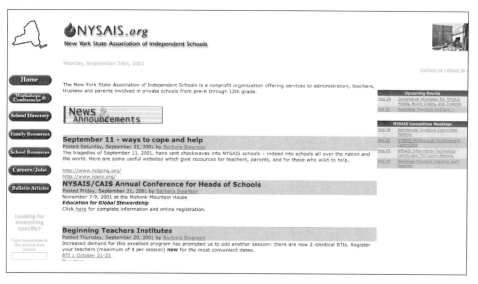

NYSAIS website home page, September 24, 2001

and teacher shortages," the Advocacy Initiative planned to promote its message to the general public, opinion leaders, prospective teachers, and families with school-age children. While
the board decided to support the initiative for a year, it asked
Executive Director Fred Calder to express some reservations to
NAIS President Pat Bassett.[4]

Another example of NYSAIS's maturity as an organization
was its willingness to make decisions regardless of what others in the independent school world were doing—and then seeing the wisdom of those decisions borne out. At the November
6, 2002 board meeting, much discussion centered on whether
NAIS could or even should be an accrediting body. With admi-
rable objectivity, Lois Bailey, who was serving on the NAIS subcommittee that was exploring this possibility, presented the
options and ramifications for NYSAIS. The minutes reflected
an adult sense of restraint: "The general consensus was that we
need to be cautious about where this is going."[5]

The 2000s were a decade of intense financial seesawing, and world events had a dramatic effect on both the resources and expenses of New York independent schools, as reflected in these minutes from the board's April 2003 meeting: "Fred is beginning to hear some softening in enrollment and leveling off of fund raising, nothing alarming, just moderate. Trends: a few schools are seeing slight increases in attrition; a number of schools are interviewing when they hadn't in previous years; there are more financial aid requests from present parents."[6]

Leadership transitions are inevitable for associations, just as they are for schools. Such was the case for our association in June 2003, when Calder let the board know that he planned to retire, effective June 2007, and the wheels were set in motion to prepare for this major transition. Also in 2003, the board bid farewell to Gordon Clem after his unprecedented twenty years of service to the Professional Development Committee.[7]

NYSAIS's growing expertise attracted the attention of other state organizations, and in 2003 Ron Goldblatt, executive director of the Maryland Association of Independent Schools (MAIS), "visited Fred to find out 'how we do what we do,'" according to board minutes. "Fred considers this a great compliment since, in his opinion, Ron is one of the finest executive directors in the country. Point of interest from Fred: the origins of these associations are interesting. NYSAIS grew out of the Packer Collegiate case and was begun by heads of schools, Maryland was a combination of heads of schools and teachers. Currently, one-third of the Maryland board is faculty. Another interesting comparison: NYSAIS has 165 member schools and Maryland has 116 members. However, we have the same budget. Clearly, our dues schedule is well below market."[7]

While financial wherewithal does not automatically signify adulthood status, it certainly does not hurt. In January 2004, the board was understandably pleased to learn from the Treasurer's Report that the association had an excess of $1 million in reserves. Much of this revenue could be attributed to Barbara Swanson's strong professional development programs, which had attracted over 2,500 participants the previous year. At the same board meeting, it was announced that Andrew McLaren— a longtime NYSAIS volunteer who had served in many different positions for over 30 years—would join the staff as associate executive director, as part of Calder's eventual transition from NYSAIS.[8] It was announced at the following board meeting that the NYSAIS Principles of Good Practice for Professional Development would be included in the evaluation manual and posted on the website for all member schools. The minutes also noted that "Barbara was completing her twentieth year, and although she was recognized at Mohonk, [Fred] wanted the minutes to reflect that she is the most accomplished, informed professional development person in the nation!"[9]

Almost halfway through the first decade of the 2000s— about the same time that *Independent School* magazine was celebrating its sixty-fifth year—Calder offered a statement of principles in the *NYSAIS Bulletin* of December, 2004. His essay "The Meaning of Association" is a perfect model for schools and other associations to follow, and it states in part:

> Associations like NYSAIS exist in the wake of Ben Franklin's warning that we either hang together or we hang alone . . . Each generation must defend its principles. Today NYSAIS schools stand firmly on the issue of "required" high-stakes testing, believing that education, in its essence, is not training. Your association maintains a substantial reserve fund for the day when forces from any quarter challenge what we believe to be our rights.

Associations like NYSAIS exist in the wake of Ben Franklin's warning that we either hang together or we hang alone . . . Each generation must defend its principles. Today NYSAIS schools stand firmly on the issue of "required" high-stakes testing, believing that education, in its essence, is not training.

—Fred Calder, third NYSAIS executive director

> There is no doubt that once again our schools will band together in the face of mindless or arbitrary intervention from any source. For it is in the end our freedom to construe our educational programs as we see fit, always, of course, respecting the needs and opinions of our communities . . . The strength of NYSAIS relies also on standards that we can exhibit confidently to the outside world . . . That our schools as a group are enormously strengthened by what is at bottom moral leadership is beyond debate. Let it never subside.[10]

At the 2005 opening board meeting, Calder reported that "he was having a great time working with Andrew McLaren and that they naturally fell into the division of responsibilities for the organization. Andrew on his part said that he was having an 'indecently good time'!"[11] At the next board meeting, which McLaren attended in place of Calder, the minutes reflected the following: "Andrew gave us an eloquent overview of his impressions during this past year of his visits to the amazing variety of schools that make up NYSAIS. In addition to the many and varied qualities that characterize our schools, everywhere he went he was left with a sense of the power of the accreditation process, the value of Heads serving as trustees at other schools, and a fear of a salary 'arms' race. In all, it was an incredible year for him, and for us."[12] It was noted that the " 'Nonpublic' schools have changed their name to the NYS Coalition of Private and Religious Schools. Everyone was tired of being 'non' something; we are private and have nothing to do with the government."[13]

At the close of 2005, Calder reported that the association was very healthy, with 173 member schools serving 73,126 children statewide. At the same time, discussions were in full swing with the board regarding school choice, including vouchers and tax credits. Calder was authorized to look into the lead school-choice advocacy program, Teach N.Y.S. The Education Alliance for Children in New York State, and the impending implications for the association.[14]

In January 2006, Calder read his official letter of resignation to the board, with his retirement scheduled to begin at the end of the 2007 academic year. Faced with the challenge of filling Calder's sizable shoes, the board immediately formed a search committee and began planning the transition process. At a special meeting of the board on June 28, 2006, the trustees voted unanimously to offer the executive director position to Elizabeth "Penney" Riegelman, head of Newark Academy in Livingston, New Jersey.[15] Riegelman accepted the position as the fourth executive director of NYSAIS with enthusiasm and began the transition process with Calder.

With much careful thought (and some deft diplomacy), the association navigated around NAIS's drive to create its own accreditation process for its member schools, while at the same time enthusiastically supporting NAIS's decision to hold its 2008 annual conference in New York City. With the theme of "Schools of the Future: Embracing the Educational ReNAIS-sance," the conference would be held at Radio City Music Hall and the Hilton Hotel. Already in full-speed-ahead mode, Swanson agreed to serve on the conference task force, and helped put together an impressive roster of speakers, including Sir Ken Robinson and author Daniel Pink, both of whom would pack Radio City Music Hall.

The minutes from the April 2007 board meeting, Calder's last, included his valedictory executive director's report: "Fred spent some time reflecting on his forty-nine years in independent school education. It has been hugely rewarding and satisfying and he must admit that he has certainly had bad days, but never bad weeks. The number one thing we need to protect in independent schools is the power to act." [16] McLaren—a NYSAIS family member who had done just about everything in the organization from professional development work to serving as board president and secretary and ultimately as acting executive director—had worked with several executive directors. He told me, "I knew Steve [Hinrichs] quite well, and I think he probably was more in the nitty-gritty of things than Fred was. I think what Fred tended to do as his modus operandi was to reserve for himself the [big] decisions, [the ones] which nobody else could make. I think that was his theory of leadership." [17]

After Calder's twenty-one years of service to the association, its member schools, and the independent school community, the family he cared for said goodbye and saluted him at a gala in his honor on April 18, 2007. At his last board meeting, Calder eloquently said, "Earnestness begins when we take issues seriously, and then take ourselves *too* seriously at the same time." He then expressed his deep gratitude to the board for many years of satisfying work, and said, "Boards should have two qualities: a plethora of good judges to determine what's impor-

tant and what's not, and no personal agenda." He complimented
the board on both counts and said
it had been a pleasure and a privilege to work with them.[18]

In my wide-ranging inter-
view with Calder in January
2014, he had this to say about
leaving NYSAIS: "There's an old
saying that you should always
leave the party while you're still
having fun. But there's a corol-
lary that I figured out lately: You
should always leave the party
while others are still having fun
with you. *You* may be having fun,
but you've got to make sure that

Exec. Director Penney Riegelman

other people are still having fun with you." Calder now divides
the year between Ohio and Lake Placid, and devotes his time to
school consulting, volunteer work, and playing bridge.[19]

At her first board meeting on November 7, 2007, Riegelman's initial assignment from the board was to seek a change in
the association's charter to include accreditation of preschools.
This undertaking would give her the opportunity to introduce
herself to legislators and become familiar with the capitol community. She also attended the fall state and regional association
executives' Independent School Association Network (ISANet)
meeting. There she learned that NAIS would no longer require
its member schools to be part of a state or regional association.
It was felt that this would not impact NYSAIS because of the
association's strength, particularly in the areas of accreditation,
professional development, and athletics.[20]

The global financial crisis of 2007–08—considered by many economists to be the worst financial crisis since the Great Depression—posed a significant challenge for NYSAIS member schools. Budgets, investments, enrollment, fundraising, and housing were just a few of the areas affected. It is worth including two brief accounts of what happened, the first from *Wikipedia* and the second by Patric H. Hendershott and Kevin Villani of the Cato Institute:

> It resulted in the threat of total collapse of large financial institutions, the bailout of banks by national governments, and downturns in stock markets around the world. In many areas, the housing market also suffered, resulting in evictions, foreclosure, and prolonged unemployment. The crisis played a significant role in the failure of key businesses, declines in consumer wealth estimated in trillions of U.S. dollars, and a downturn in economic activity leading to the 2008–2012 global recession and contributing to the European sovereign-debt crisis. The active phase of the crisis, which manifested as a liquidity crisis, can be dated from August 9, 2007, when BNP Paribas terminated withdrawals from three hedge funds citing "a complete evaporation of liquidity."[21]
>
> The current narrative regarding the 2008 systemic financial system collapse is that numerous seemingly unrelated events occurred in unregulated or underregulated markets, requiring widespread bailouts of actors across the financial spectrum, from mortgage borrowers to investors in money market funds. The Financial Crisis Inquiry Commission, created by the U.S. Congress to investigate the causes of the crisis, promotes this politically convenient narrative, and the 2010 Dodd-Frank Act

operationalizes it by completing the progressive extension of federal protection and regulation of banking and
finance that began in the 1930s so that it now covers
virtually all financial activities, including hedge funds and
proprietary trading. The Dodd-Frank Act further charges
the newly created Financial Stability Oversight Council,
made up of politicians, bureaucrats, and university pro-
fessors, with preventing a subsequent systemic crisis.[22]

Amid the looming financial crisis and its own leadership
transition, the association continued to look forward in 2008,
mounting a yearlong strategic planning process. One key decision was to shift its fiscal year (from September through August
to July through June) to aid in budgeting. At the same time,
the athletic executive committee was tested at every turn. The
challenges were many: eligibility, scheduling, rules and vari-
ances, deadlines, and postseason play, not to mention overseeing referees, coaches, and players. In an effort to keep up with
the constant demands for consistency, clarification, and excep-
tions, the committee continued to examine its communications
procedures, which included:

- Providing a philosophical statement on postseason
  play;
- Creating a new handbook for heads and admissions
  directors; and
- Posting athletic information about deadlines and
  reminders on the NYSAIS website.

Riegelman encouraged the board to undertake an annual
self-evaluation, as well as an evaluation of the executive director. It was a policy the board readily embraced, given that it was
already an accreditation criteria for its member school boards;

it was also an opportunity for the association to serve as a strong role model.[23] Swanson found herself devoting more time and energy to improving the functionality of the NYSAIS website—a reflection of the Internet's explosive impact on communications, not only in the independent school community but all over the world.

As part of a strategic planning process, Riegelman provided the board with a quick overview of the recent survey of NYSAIS heads, which had yielded an impressive 52 percent return. Among the findings: School heads gave universally high ratings to the professional development and accreditation programs; they also made consistent pleas for regular governance activities in many areas, including for new and returning heads, board chairs, new board members, and heads of finance committees.[24]

The association entered the last year of the decade with much on its plate. It began to explore online learning, an exploding form of education for member schools. Its working strategic plan stipulated a number of goals, including:

Goal One: Provide member services and counsel, at no additional cost, to aid schools in meeting their individual missions.

Goal Two: Ensure the strong, effective governance of NYSAIS schools.

Goal Three: Strengthen the network of NYSAIS schools, so that all schools are supported and served by all of the Association's programs.[25]

The most significant development of 2009 was the news that Executive Director Penney Riegelman intended to step down. At the June board meeting, "President Richard Bryan acknowledged that this is Penney's last meeting, pointing out that Penney took on a large task of moving the association through a difficult transition. He commended her accomplishments, including: getting Board Committees established and running well for the future, clarifying NYSAIS's role in Albany, reaching out to many schools, changing auditors, and tightening up the financial systems. She spearheaded the Strategic Plan and nudged NYSAIS forward. He recognized that Penney is leaving NYSAIS on account of two cherished values: the importance of family, and the importance of running schools."[26]

Bryan also thanked the Executive Director Search Committee for its hard work and efficiency, which had resulted in the appointment of Mark W. Lauria, Ph.D. as NYSAIS's fifth executive director. Lauria's broad experience—as a middle school teacher, principal, and assistant superintendent in the California public school system; as a thirteen-year head of the Foothill Country Day School in Claremont, California; and as president of the California Association of Independent Schools board of directors—made him an ideal candidate to lead the association into the second decade of the 2000s.

Looking back on the executive director transitions of the late 2000s, it is evident that Riegelman played a vital role in helping the association move on—literally and figuratively—following twenty-one years of Calder's distinctive leadership, which had strategically guided the association from the preadolescent years through adolescence and into adulthood. It was now up to Lauria to further NYSAIS's growth, stability, and innovation, in partnership with Swanson, Bailey, the trustees, and hundreds of volunteers. NYSAIS's leadership transition was not unlike what NAIS went through, when, following the long tenure of President John Esty, it hired Peter Relic to oversee the association's move from Boston to Washington, D.C., before passing the baton to Pat Bassett.

Executive Director Dr. Mark Lauria

Surely one of the biggest changes of the 2000s—and one that very much continues today—was the growing role of technology in NYSAIS member schools. That change can be seen in hiring practices: many member schools hired faculty to teach technology courses, and computer programmers to oversee their information technology (IT) infrastructure.

Increasingly, member schools needed to teach their students an under-the-hood understanding of computers and how to control them through programming. In a sense, education in technology has come full circle, from the early years of programming using Basic, Logo, Pascal, and HTML to today when students are learning how to design applications for smartphones. This comeback of computer programming instruction was front-page news in the May 11, 2014 *New York Times*. "Reading, Writing, Arithmetic, and Now Coding" by Matt Richtel describes a "national educational movement in computer coding instruction that is growing at Internet speeds."[28]

Swanson's early focus on technology meant that NYSAIS never skipped a beat, leading the way for member schools with email, data retrieval, and website presentation. With the aid of member school IT directors and librarians, the association sought out state-of-the-art technology to support schools, pro-

THE EVOLUTION OF TECHNOLOGY

Because we have been so consumed by technology over the past twenty years, a stroll down memory lane—specifically, the video game aisle—may help to put our association's technology growth into historical perspective:

1971 Oregon Trail
1972 Pong
1980 Pac-Man
1981 Donkey Kong
1984 Tetris
1985 Nintendo Entertainment Center
1988 John Madden Football
1989 Nintendo Game Boy
1989 SimCity
1990 Electronic version of Solitaire
1992 Dune II
1993 Mortal Kombat
1995 Sony PlayStation
1997 IBM's Deep Blue chess computer triumphs over
      world champion Gary Kasparov
2001 Microsoft Xbox
2006 Nintendo Wii
2008 World of Warcraft
2009 FarmVille and Angry Birds
2010 Minecraft[27]

grams, media centers, and libraries, and to facilitate marketing and data retrieval. Recognizing that the demand for technology would only continue to grow, Lauria decided that the time had come for NYSAIS to hire a staff member focused exclusively on technology. Now, with its own director of technology, NYSAIS can offer an interactive website that supports an association-wide online community portal, webinars, online registrations, extensive executive director Twitter feeds, and live streaming of conferences so members who cannot attend an event can view keynote speakers and lectures right from their offices and homes.

By the end of the decade, the association was bursting with ideas and a spirit ready for growth. The assessment that Lauria, Swanson, and the Professional Development Committee conducted of the many services being provided to member schools reflected that spirit. In addition to various board committees and the commission on accreditation, NYSAIS supported close to a dozen major institutes and initiatives, including:

- Conference Planning Committees
  - o Annual Heads Conference
  - o Technology & Library Media Conference
  - o Diversity Conference
  - o Admissions
  - o Development
  - o Division Heads
  - o Heads' Assistants
- Diversity Committee
- Business Affairs Council
- Beginning Teachers Institute
- Experienced Teachers Institute

The Professional Development Committee was eager to support the work of both the Diversity Committee and Technology Committee. Swanson proposed that these three committees hold a tri-committee meeting toward the end of the school year to compare goals and exchange ideas. By so doing, the Professional Development Committee could support the needs of individual committee through workshops and conference planning. This gathering of committee members proved to be fruitful for all involved.

At about the same time, the association created a network of professional development liaisons. Each member school chose a faculty member to serve as the professional development coordinator at her/his school and as the direct link with NYSAIS workshops and programs. Each fall, NYSAIS held a planning workshop for all the liaisons, so they could discuss issues, challenges, and successes, and gain insights on how they could use the association to better support their school.

One fall evening in 2009, while sitting on the porch at the Rensselaerville Institute Conference Center in the midst of a BTI, Swanson, Lauria, and I began thinking about the success of the tri-committee meetings and how we might expand this collaborative concept to include all committees. Lauria proposed that NYSAIS host an annual three-day residential think tank that would include one or two representatives from each committee.

The first think tank was held in June 2010 and proved a great success. It provided time for all the participants to exchange accomplishments and challenges with one another, thus building a stronger support system for the many volunteers who make up these committees. One idea generated in this and successive think tanks was the Emerging Leaders Institute (ELI). Catering to the burgeoning pool of teachers who aspired to become leaders within the independent school community, ELI selected its first sixteen-person cohort from nominations

NYSAIS's first Think Tank, 2010

submitted by heads of member schools. It was synonymous with building a "farm team" of future leaders—educators who would become division heads, administrative directors, or eventually heads of school.

At the November 3, 2010 board meeting, Lauria reported that NYSAIS would be moving to Albany. Located at 17 Elk Street in downtown Albany within walking distance of the state capitol and legislative office building, the NYSAIS office could not have been more centrally located. Lauria proposed that all March board meetings would take place at the NYSAIS office. Working with the trustees and NYSAIS's lobbyist, he coordinated annual visits to each trustee's respective state representative and senator in his or her capitol office.

The idea of cross-program collaboration continued to percolate, and in 2011 it was decided that a group of representatives from each committee and institute would plan to meet on a regular basis throughout the school year with a culminating meeting at the annual think tank. This new body, called the

Council for Professional Learning and Collaboration (CPLC), was instituted into the NYSAIS bylaws by a vote of the board on November 2, 2011. The CPLC mission states:

> The Council for Professional Learning and Collaboration (CPLC) provides a platform for communication and coordination such that NYSAIS professional learning programs meet the ever-changing needs of our diverse community of schools.
>
> To support the mission, the commission will:
> - Create collaborative relationships among NYSAIS professional groups who plan programs such as conferences, workshops, institutes, and online learning.
> - Use feedback from the accreditation process to inform the work of this Council.
> - Provide guidance and leadership for improving practices within the professional groups.
> - Promote strategic and generative reflection.

In the early stages of CPLC's development, the metaphor used most often was that of breaking down the silos (individual committees) and building one single farm of professional learning and collaboration. As a standing committee of the board of trustees, the CPLC would include representation from the following "silos" that would soon become a collaborative working farm:

- Athletic Association
- Business Affairs Council
- Conference Planning Committees
  - o Admissions
  - o Annual Heads

- o Athletics
- o Brain
- o Diversity Practitioners (formerly known as Diversity)
- o Division Heads
- o Early Childhood
- o Heads' Assistants
- o Institutional Advancement (formerly known as Development)
- o NYSAIS Education and Information Technology (NEIT) (formerly known as Technology Committee)
- Diversity Committee
- Institutes
  - o Beginning Teachers
  - o Emerging Leaders
  - o Experienced Teachers
- NYSAIS Education and Information Technology (NEIT) (formerly known as the Technology Committee)
- Professional Development Committee
- Trustee Training Workshops
- Webinars

Truly, 2011 was an exceptional year; so much was accomplished. At the January 19 board meeting, a summation was given on the work that had been done over the previous twenty-two months in preparation for revising the *NYSAIS Manual for Evaluation and Accreditation*. This ongoing work culminated in the development of a draft by the end of August. The major revisions to the manual included a much-expanded governance section; a more structured educational program section; criteria that are front and center in the process; and a leaner, more structured format. At the annual meeting in November, printed copies of the new manual (Version 3.1) were distributed to all trustees; Lauria acknowledged the many volunteers who contributed to its content, particularly the members of the Commission on Accreditation.

Caring for the extended family of member schools remained a priority for the association. To assist those member schools that could not otherwise afford to attend NYSAIS workshops and conferences, Lauria and the board decided to underwrite the schools' registration fees. On November 2, Lauria reported to the board that thirteen schools had already participated in the financial aid offered for attending conferences and workshops in 2011, providing thirty-six people with professional development experiences they would otherwise not have had.

In the face of escalating medical insurance costs, Lauria and the Business Affairs Council were determined to create a consortium for member schools to help mitigate premium costs. By presenting a larger pool of participants, individual school costs could be reduced considerably. After much work and research by the Health Consortium Task Force, on January 19, 2011 the NYSAIS board of trustees voted to form NYSAIS Operations, Inc., which would be its own 501(c)(6) nonprofit organization (while still inextricably linked to the NYSAIS 501(c)(3) nonprofit corporation). Using the same governance structure, including the NYSAIS trustees and staff, this new entity would oversee the consortium's insurance program, which would dedicate its operations to negotiating with and hiring insurance companies to serve those member schools with over fifty employees. Such high-level "generative thinking"—which focuses on generating fresh ideas and solutions—could only come from a thoroughly adult organization.

Another example of this adult generative thinking came when Lauria and several members of the NYSAIS Board of Trustees wanted to provide more critical governance and leadership support to schools, particularly as it applied to accreditation recommendations. If ever there was an area needing regular support in our member schools, it is our school boards and trustees. A two-year process of research and planning resulted in the Experienced Leaders Advising Schools (ELAS) program, which would provide high-impact, low-cost consulting to member schools by employing retired school heads and administrators to "ed-vise" schools on issues of governance, leadership, finances, enrollment, or other administrative needs. The program was adopted and funded by the Board of Trustees in the spring of 2012, and the first "ed-visement" took place the following summer. This new program would be especially useful during the accreditation process, when ELAS could provide expert and affordable support as member schools sought to implement major recommendations.

The decision was made to hold the 2011 Heads Annual Conference together with the heads from CAIS and the New Jersey Association of Independent Schools (NJAIS). It was further agreed by the three associations to hold a tri-state conference format every three years, because, as Lauria later described it, "Building bridges with other organizations is important, and building really good, strong relationships with the tri-state [has been] accomplished through the tri-state heads conference and the tri-state

business managers conference."[29] The Conference Planning Committee, made up of representatives from the three associations, provided for a very special presentation in the "kickoff" year. Here is the description from the conference program:

Session 4 – The Music Paradigm
Conductor: Maestro Roger Nierenberg

The Music Paradigm uses a symphony orchestra as a metaphor for any dynamic organization, particularly one dealing with a period of exceptional challenge or change: a merger, a restructuring, new leadership, change initiatives, stretch performance goals, and many more. The session is a high-impact learning experience, a powerful personal and team journey, and exciting instructional entertainment. The session provides a highly memorable group experience that generates fresh insights and lessons that become part of the organization's dialogue and culture.[30]

Participants at the well-attended session were treated to a thirty-two-piece string orchestra playing Tchaikovsky's "Serenade for Strings in C major, Op. 48," interspersed with commentary from the conductor, explaining how leading a school is akin to conducting an orchestra. The conductor and musicians received a long standing ovation of appreciation.

The revised bylaws presented at the May 31, 2012 board meeting required that all full member, not-for-profit schools must undergo a NYSAIS accreditation. In his executive director's report, Lauria stated that the 2011 repeal of the Metropolitan Transportation Authority (MTA) payroll tax had already resulted in savings for a large percentage of NYSAIS schools. At that same meeting, there was discussion about adding funding to the NYSAIS budget for an assistant director of accreditation to assist Bailey with the steadily expanding process.[31]

The board was presented with outside accrediting agencies recommended for formal recognition by the NYSAIS board. Following a discussion, all agreed that the accrediting agencies were acceptable to NYSAIS for the purpose of partnership and recognition of their accredited schools. The NYSAIS bylaws state that if a for-profit school wishes to become a member, it must be accredited by an accrediting body that is recognized by NYSAIS. There was a motion to recognize the following accrediting agencies:

- Council of International Schools
- Middle States Association of Colleges and Schools
- American Montessori Society
- Association of Waldorf Schools of North America
- Independent Schools Inspectorate[32]

In the winter of 2013, NAIS announced that the distinguished author and educator, John Chubb, Ph.D., would succeed Pat Bassett as president of NAIS, beginning in July 2013. Chubb is the author of numerous books, the most recent being *The Best Teachers in the World: Why We Don't Have Them and How We Could* (Hoover Institution Press Publication, 2012). Remember what Calder said back in the February 1991 *NYSAIS Bulletin* about Chubb and his book: "Virtually everyone seems to have read, or read about John Chubb and Terry Moe's *Politics, Markets and America's Schools*"?

On December 14, 2012, an unthinkable tragedy unfolded in a small Connecticut town, leaving an indelible stain on the entire school world for years to come. After first shooting his mother, twenty-year old Adam Lanza proceeded to Sandy Hook Elementary School in Newtown, Connecticut, where he shot

Lois Bailey Tribute 2012

twenty schoolchildren and six adults, before taking his own life. The deadliest mass shooting at a high school or elementary school in U.S. history, this event understandably instigated a wave of school security measures within NYSAIS and at schools throughout the world. The NYSAIS Accreditation Commission mobilized to review health and safety criteria in the accreditation process to make sure all member schools incorporated appropriate measures to protect their students, staff, and faculty.[33]

In the midst of this horrific tragedy, a beacon of inspiration shone brightly within the NYSAIS community. At the 2012 annual meeting and at the its May 30, 2013 meeting, the board recognized Lois Bailey following her retirement after twenty-five years of service to NYSAIS (1987 to July 2012). She accomplished so much for schools during her tenure, providing endless support to volunteers and dedicating untold hours to making the accreditation process one of the best in the country. A bench at the Emma Willard School—outside the former NYSAIS office—holds a plaque with a most apropos inscription:

"Honoring Lois S. Bailey: Dedicated and insightful advocate for the accreditation process, and steadfast friend to the NYSAIS community of schools. New York Association of Independent Schools, November 2012." Everyone in the NYSAIS community knew that Bailey did the work of two people, a fact that was confirmed when Lauria hired two people to oversee Bailey's responsibilities within one year of her departure.

The very next year, Bailey's longtime colleague and friend, Barbara Swanson, was also recognized for her thirty years of service and devotion to the association at the November 2013 annual heads conference. Inscribed on a plaque on a bench at Mohonk Mountain House—her home away from home—is a Twitter-size inscription for an Internet-size administrator, which seems fitting for someone who advanced technology the way she did: "In honor of Barbara B. Swanson, who has dedicated with intelligence, good humor, and rare grace, 30 years to NYSAIS. Her work has transformed the lives of innumerable educators who, in turn shaped the lives of students. . . . With deepest appreciation from the NYSAIS Community, November 6, 2013." At this point Swanson has said that she has no immediate plans for leaving her NYSAIS family. How fortunate for NYSAIS.

When you compare NYSAIS in its infancy to its adult years, the fundamental essence of the association remains strikingly consistent. Take, for instance, the association's original charter and compare it with the most recently revised and adopted bylaws:

> The purpose of the organization shall be to promote the independence and well-being of and public regard for the independent schools of the State of New York; to safeguard the interests of these schools in the matter of legislation and regulation; to foster mutually beneficial

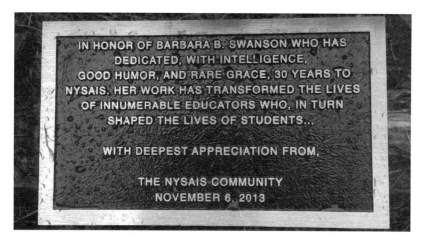

IN HONOR OF BARBARA B. SWANSON WHO HAS
DEDICATED, WITH INTELLIGENCE,
GOOD HUMOR, AND RARE GRACE, 30 YEARS TO
NYSAIS. HER WORK HAS TRANSFORMED THE LIVES
OF INNUMERABLE EDUCATORS WHO, IN TURN
SHAPED THE LIVES OF STUDENTS...

WITH DEEPEST APPRECIATION FROM,

THE NYSAIS COMMUNITY
NOVEMBER 6, 2013

Barbara Swanson Tribute 2013

relations with the New York State Education Department
and other educational agencies; to serve as the New
York State member association of the National Association of Independent Schools; to assist member schools
in maintaining standards of excellence; to encourage
activities for the purpose of keeping our education work
updated and current; to provide service and leadership
to the communities of which we are a part.
—NYSAIS Constitution of the original Charter granted
by the N.Y. State Board of Regents October 26, 1968

The purpose of the Association shall be to promote the
cause of education in general; to promote in particular
the independence and well-being of, and public regard
for, the independent schools of the State of New York;
to safeguard the interests of these schools and inform
and counsel them in matters of legislation and regulation; to foster mutually beneficial relations with the New
York State Education Department, the National Asso-

ciation of Independent Schools, and other educational associations; through evaluation and accreditation to assist member schools in developing and maintaining standards of excellence; to promote professional growth of teachers, administrators, and trustees through workshops, conferences, and exchanges; to facilitate the development of cooperative projects among member schools and between member schools and public schools; through publications and visitations to inform the membership about significant practices and developments in independent education; to provide such other services as will benefit the member schools and the communities they serve.

—NYSAIS bylaws amended and approved by the Board of Trustees on May 31, 2012

Remaining true to its purpose and mission is critical to any organization; never fearing to extend itself in exploration and growth, yet knowing when to circle the wagons so that the organization and its members will be protected from significant incursions. The association's strength does not rest in its assets of over $2 million, impressive as those are; it rests in the people who provide service on a daily basis to the 194 member schools that serve more than 79,000 students. The lion's share of that service can be glimpsed in these astounding 2013-2014 statistics: sixty-eight professional development events and twenty-one residential events, serving 3,450 participants; twenty ten-year accreditation visits and eleven five-year review visits by over 215 volunteer visiting committee members, with the support of twenty NYSAIS accreditation commissioners; and thirteen regional meetings serving over 190 participants throughout the state.

As a mature adult—now serving almost as a parent to its family of member schools—the association marches steadily forward, always aiming for the highest standards. When I mentioned this notion of NYSAIS being a family to Andrew McLaren, he stated, "That is an interesting question. I've certainly seen it in a number of iterations, going back to Ap Mason, who probably [originated that sense] of NYSAIS as a family. I think the two strands are woven together. It's definitely an organization that has clarity of purpose and a reason for being as an organization. But the desire that people have to contribute to NYSAIS is, I think, actually a kind of idealized family. One of the things that amused me when I was working for NYSAIS was that during those three years, I didn't have a difficult conversation with anybody. It was not like being a head of school, where I would have a different kind of family conversation, in which we bickered with each other: the generations would feud, all the teachers would say, 'Look at what this idiot head is saying,' and parents would complain. With NYSAIS, there was none of that." [29]

Individual staff members and volunteers may retire and move on from NYSAIS, but based on its past and its present, it seems clear that NYSAIS will continue to attract new generations of leaders and remain a hard-working advocate for its member schools. Recently, Lauria commented on what the association has accomplished during his five-year tenure and what he envisions for the association's immediate future. First the accomplishments:

- Moving the office from Schenectady to Albany, to place us in a better position for lobbying.
- Putting regional meetings in place. NYSAIS had never done regional meetings; now we've done them for five years. It's a way for myself and the entire NYSAIS staff

One of the things that people have asked me is, "Is it just about change?" For me, it's never just about change. It's always about continuous improvement. Change for change's sake is crazy. Change is for continuous improvement or continuously looking at what it is you're doing and how do you make it better. That is what is important.

—Executive Director Dr. Mark Lauria

to listen to what's going on in the different regions, to talk with those member schools and give NYSAIS a presence again, strengthening that fabric throughout the state.

- Revising the accreditation manual. Not only did we restructure the way we do accreditation, we also restructured the way the commission on accreditation works.

- Creating the Healthcare Consortium and forming NYSAIS Operations. That was a huge accomplishment.

- Expanding our use of technology, which enhances the way we do business now. We've created a virtual world for NYSAIS, and that's a major change to the way we run the association—such as how our virtual staff meetings work. We've also done two upgrades to the website over the past five years—one in 2010 and one in 2014. All of our records are much clearer.

Everything is in the cloud. We have a really nice system for organizing everything.

- Creating a strong sense of community within our association through our professional development programs. The NYSAIS name is widely recognized, so when you talk to teachers or administrators, they know NYSAIS. They have been to a NYSAIS event. The fabric of NYSAIS is really apparent throughout the entire state. Everybody gets it.

Now the immediate future:

- Continuing to build relationships and strengthen the fabric of our community. NYSAIS sees itself, and rightly so, as a community of educators. I think it's because of the relationships we build at our conferences, particularly our residential conferences.
- Continuing responsiveness to our schools in both accreditation and professional development. We'll see a really strong evolution of the accreditation process as we begin to tackle the idea of online learning and what that means. We're really wrestling with issues like what is a school? What are the fundamental components that need to be there for it to be a school? Before it was a building. In the online world, that's not necessarily the case.
- Making sure that the staff is out there listening and participating, making contacts and creating connections. While we sustain these connections through our video-conferencing and things like that, we create them through our face-to-face interactions. To me that's the balance.

NYSAIS takes its message to Times Square, May 23, 2013.

- Making continuous improvements. One of the things that people have asked me is, 'Is it just about change?' For me, it's never just about change. It's always about continuous improvement. Change for change's sake is crazy. Change is for continuous improvement or continuously looking at what it is you're doing and how do you make it better. That is what is important.[29]

Like any family, watching over the growth and development of its children is all-consuming—as it should be. The ebb and flow of connectedness is what cements any strong family. Whether it is working one-on-one with a small upstate school or proudly showcasing member school names and pictures in the heart of Times Square, NYSAIS is committed to watching over its schools, tending to their needs, supporting them during their vulnerable years, protecting when danger lurks, helping them to grow and embrace their independence. That *is* the design.

ACKNOWLEDGMENTS

Whenever books are written, there is most certainly a family of support given to the author. This is surely the case with *Independent by Design: A History of the New York State Association of Independent Schools*. The importance of a good editor was key to my being able to write, write, and write and not lose sight of the details and continuity of the story. Beth Brosnan was by my side in editing, advising, and making sure the writing was always meant for the reader. Also, my thanks go to Susan Gold, who designed the cover and inside layout with much artistic care.

To the many proofreaders and fact checkers—Jim Adams, Richard Barter, Fred Calder, and Mark Lauria—I give thanks. And a note of appreciation to those individuals whom I interviewed along the way: Lois Bailey, Fred Calder, Tom Hogan, Mark Lauria, Andrew McLaren, and Barbara Swanson.

A note of acknowledgement goes to the NYSAIS staff—Andrew Cooke, Maria Flores, Judy Sheridan, George Swain, Barbara Swanson, and Diana Wahrlich—for being ever ready to answer my questions and provide support; and especially to Mark Lauria for giving me the opportunity to write this history and providing encouragement all along the way.

Finally, my trusty sidekick, Chris Peters, herself a longtime educator, was always willing and able to take notes, set up an index, transcribe data from one document to another, adjust our family schedule to accommodate last-minute deadlines, and offer whatever support she could to me and the project. To her, I offer much love and appreciation.

NOTES

INTRODUCTION

1 U.S. Department of Education ED.gov website

2 *Five Life Stages of Nonprofit Organizations*, Judith Sharken Simon, Fieldstone Alliance, 2001

CHAPTER ONE Birth & Infant Years: 1940s and 1950s

1 Demobilization of United States armed forces after WWII, Wikipedia

2 "Since 1925 the state and private schools . . ." Fred Calder in his February–April 1998 *Bulletin*, "The Roots of Independence," p. 24

3 From Amazon.com Editorial Review section on *Dr. Spock's Baby and Child Care*

4 Women's Liberation Movement website

5 Minutes to January 18, 1949 1st Annual Meeting

6 Minutes to October 26, 1948 Executive Committee Meeting

7 *Independent School* magazine, Spring 2006

8 Minutes to January 17, 1950 2nd Annual Meeting

9 From the Writer's Almanac January 1, 2014 website

10 Minutes to January 16, 1951 3rd Annual Meeting

11 Minutes to January 15, 1952 4th Annual Meeting

12 Minutes to January 20, 1953 5th Annual Meeting

13 Eisenhower Archives website

14 Kenrick, John, "History of the Musical Stage 1950s I: When Broadway Ruled" website

15 Minutes to January 19, 1954 6th Annual Meeting

16 Official Elvis Presley website

17 History of *Brown v. Board of Education*, United States Courts website

18 Minutes to November 1, 1955 Executive Committee Meeting

19 Minutes to January 18, 1955 7th Annual Meeting

20 Minutes to January 17, 1956 8th Annual Meeting

21 Minutes to January 15, 1957 9th Annual Meeting

22 NASA History Homepage

23 Minutes to January 21, 1958 10th Annual Meeting

24 Minutes to April 15, 1958 Executive Committee Meeting

25 Minutes to October 14, 1958 Executive Committee Meeting

26 Minutes to January 20, 1959 11th Annual Meeting

CHAPTER TWO Early Childhood Years: 1960s

1 About.com 20th Century History, 1960s Timeline website

2 Brosnan, Michael, "Sorting It Out," *Independent School*, Spring 2006, pp. 80-89

3 Minutes to January 19, 1960 12th Annual Meeting

4 Minutes to January 17, 1961 13th Annual Meeting

5 Minutes to January 15, 1962 14th Annual Meeting

6 Minutes to March 2, 1962 Executive Committee Meeting

7 Minutes to October 31, 1962 Executive Committee Meeting

8 "To Affect the Quality of the Day" by Ewald B. Nyquist, delivered at the Association's Annual Meeting January 14, 1963

9 Minutes to January 14, 1963 15th Annual Meeting

10 "Northeast Blackout of 1965," Wikipedia

11 "Beatles Fans Hear Yesterday Again," Allan Kozinn, *New York Times*, Feb. 2, 2014

12 Minutes to January 13, 1964 16th Annual Meeting

13 Minutes to October 5 and 6, 1964 Special Meeting

14 Minutes to November 16, 1965 17th Annual Meeting

by Date, Hawes Publications website, Revised: June 10, 2014

3   *New York Times* Number One Fiction Bestsellers Listed by Date, Hawes Publications website, Revised: June 10, 2014

4   Minutes to January 30, 1980 Board of Trustees meeting

5   Minutes to January 20, 1981 Board of Trustees meeting

6   Minutes to April 16, 1980 Board of Trustees meeting

7   Minutes to January 27, 1982 Board of Trustees meeting

8   Minutes to April 21, 1982 Board of Trustees meeting

9   Minutes to January 26, 1983 Board of Trustees meeting

10 Minutes to November 3, 1983 35th Annual Meeting

11 Calder, Frederick interview January 31, 2014

12 Hogan, Tom interview April 21, 2014

13 Obituary: Vaughn Phillips Montaigne Keith link

14 Bernhard Goetz, Wikipedia

15 Brosnan, Michael, "Sorting It Out," *Independent School*, Spring 2006, pp. 80-89

16 "Floppy disk," Wikipedia

17 Swanson, Barbara interview April 15, 2014

18 Bailey, Lois interview April 15, 2014

19 Swanson, Barbara interview April 15, 2014

20 Executive Director's Report 1981-82

21 Executive Director's Report 1983-84

22 Executive Director's Report 1984-85

23 Executive Director's Report 1985-86

24 Calder, Frederick, *Without Apology: Reflections on Independent Education*, 2007, pp. 26-27

25 Executive Director's Report 1985-86

26 Executive Director's Report 1986-87 as presented in the June 16-17, 1987 Board Minutes

27 Executive Director's Report as presented in the June 20-21, 1988 Board Minutes

28 Minutes to June 19, 1989 Board of Trustees meeting

29 Executive Director's Report 1988-89 as presented in the Minutes to June 19, 1989 Board of Trustees meeting

CHAPTER FIVE Adolescent Years: 1990s

1   "List of *Billboard* Hot 100 Number-One Singles of the 1990s," Wikipedia

2   About.com 20th Century History

3   O'Neill Grace, Catherine, "Before the World Changed: *Independent School* in the 1990s," *Independent School*, Spring 2006, pp. 90-100

4   Calder, Frederick, *Without Apology: Reflections on Independent Education*, 2007

5   Executive Director's Annual Report June 1990

6   Minutes to January 17, 1990 Board of Trustees meeting

7   Executive Director's Annual Report June 1990-91

8   Calder, Frederick, *Without Apology: Reflections on Independent Education*, 2007, p. 134

9   Relic, Peter, "School Choice ≠ Politics; School Choice = Justice," NAIS paper, 1991

10 "Statement on Aspects of Educational Choice," NYSAIS Board of Trustees, June 1991

11 "Trustee Policy Statement on NYSAIS Advisory Services," 1991-92

12 Executive Director's Annual Report June 1992-93

13 Strategic Planning Committee Report to the NYSAIS Board of Trustees, April 1994

14 Executive Director's Annual Report June 1994-95

15 Minutes to April 17, 1996 Board of Trustees meeting

16 Walsh, Brian (President of the NYSAIS Board of Trustees), letter to NYSAIS Heads, April 21, 1997

17 Minutes to June 23, 1997 Board of Trustees meeting

18 Hefferren, Aileen, Chief Executive of Prep for Prep (http://

www.prepforprep.org/), email to the author, January 22, 2014

19 Minutes to November 5, 1997 Board of Trustees meeting

20 Calder, Frederick, *Without Apology: Reflections on Independent Education*, 2007, p. 75

21 Minutes to April 21, 1999 Board of Trustees meeting

22 Minutes to June 21, 1999 Board of Trustees meeting

23 Barter, Dr. Richard, email to the author, April 25, 2014

CHAPTER SIX Adult Years: 2000s and Beyond

1 Columbine High School Massacre, Wikipedia, May 12, 2014

2 American Educational History: A Hypertext Timeline

3 Minutes to June 19, 2000 Board of Trustees meeting

4 Minutes to June 21, 2001 Board of Trustees meeting

5 Minutes to November 6, 2002 Board of Trustees meeting

6 Minutes to April 23, 2003 Board of Trustees meeting

7 Minutes to June 16, 2003 Board of Trustees meeting

8 Minutes to January 21, 2004 Board of Trustees meeting

9 Minutes to April 21, 2004 Board of Trustees meeting

10 Calder, Frederick, *Without Apology: Reflections on Independent Education*, 2007, pp. 40-41

11 Minutes to January 19, 2005 Board of Trustees meeting

12 Minutes to April 20, 2005 Board of Trustees meeting

13 Minutes to June 14, 2005 Board of Trustees meeting

14 Minutes to November 2, 2005 Board of Trustees meeting

15 Minutes to June 28, 2006 Board of Trustees special meeting

16 Minutes to April 19, 2007 Board of Trustees meeting

17 McLaren, Andrew interview June 2, 2014

18 Minutes to June 7, 2007 Board of Trustees meeting

19 Calder, Frederick interview January 31, 2014

20 Minutes to November 7, 2007 Board of Trustees meeting

21 "Financial Crisis of 2007-08," Wikipedia

22 Hendershott, Patric H. and Kevin Villani, "What Made the Financial Crisis Systemic," CATO Institute, March 6, 2012

23 Minutes to January 16, 2008 Board of Trustees meeting

24 Minutes to June 16, 2008 Board of Trustees meeting

25 Minutes to January 21, 2009 Board of Trustees meeting

26 Minutes to June 17, 2009 Board of Trustees meeting

27 International Center for the History of Electronic Games

28 Richtel, Matt, *New York Times*. "Reading, Writing, Arithmetic, and Now Coding," May 11, 2014

29 Lauria, Mark interview June 5, 2014

30 NYSAIS Conference Program, November 2, 2011

31 Minutes to May 31, 2012 Board of Trustees meeting

32 Minutes to November 6, 2013 Board of Trustees meeting

33 "Sandy Hook Elementary School Shooting," Wikipedia

REFERENCES

Simon, Judith Sharken, *Five Life Stages of Nonprofit Organizations*, Fieldstone Alliance, 2001, New York, NY

The Nonprofit Board Answer Book, Third Edition, BoardSource, Jossey-Bass, 2012, San Francisco, CA

APPENDIX A

BOARD OF TRUSTEES OFFICERS

1947
President, Paul D. Shafer, The Packer Collegiate Institute, Brooklyn
Vice President, Anne Wellington, Emma Willard School, Troy
Secretary/Treasurer, Harry E. P. Meislahn, The Albany Academy, Albany

1948
President, Paul D. Shafer, The Packer Collegiate Institute, Brooklyn
Vice President, Anne Wellington, Emma Willard School, Troy
Secretary/Treasurer, Harry E. P. Meislahn, The Albany Academy, Albany

1949
President, Paul D. Shafer, The Packer Collegiate Institute, Brooklyn
Vice President, Anne Wellington, Emma Willard School, Troy
Secretary/Treasurer, Harry E. P. Meislahn, The Albany Academy, Albany

1950
President, Paul D. Shafer, The Packer Collegiate Institute, Brooklyn
Vice President, Anne Wellington, Emma Willard School, Troy
Secretary/Treasurer, Harry E. P. Meislahn, The Albany Academy, Albany

1951
President, Paul D. Shafer, The Packer Collegiate Institute, Brooklyn
Vice President, Dorothy Brockway Osborne, The Spence School, New York
Secretary/Treasurer, Harry E. P. Meislahn, The Albany Academy, Albany

1952
President, Charles Bradlee, Pebble Hill School, DeWitt
Vice President, Helen Burtt Mason, The Berkeley Institute, Brooklyn
Secretary/Treasurer, Harry E. P. Meislahn, The Albany Academy, Albany

1953
President, Harry E. P. Meislahn, The Albany Academy, Albany
Vice President, Elizabeth Parmalee, The Calhoun School, New York
Secretary/Treasurer, Blanche Pittman, St. Agnes School, Rochester

1954
President, Harry E. P. Meislahn, The Albany Academy, Albany
Vice President, Elizabeth Parmalee, The Calhoun School, New York
Secretary/Treasurer, Blanche Pittman, St. Agnes School, Rochester

1955
President, Harry E. P. Meislahn, The Albany Academy, Albany
Vice President, Rev. Dane Kirsch, S.J. Canisius H.S., Buffalo
Secretary/Treasurer, Blanche Pittman, St. Agnes School, Rochester

1956
President, Harry E. P. Meislahn, The Albany Academy, Albany
Vice President, Rev. Dane Kirsch, S.J. Canisius H.S., Buffalo
Secretary/Treasurer, Blanche Pittman, St. Agnes School, Rochester

1957
President, J. Folwell Scull Jr., Polytechnic Preparatory Country Day School,
    Brooklyn
Vice President, Morison Brigham, DeVeaux School, Niagara Falls
Secretary/Treasurer, Clemewell Lay, Emma Willard School, Troy

1958
President, J. Folwell Scull Jr., Polytechnic Preparatory Country Day School,
    Brooklyn
Vice President, Morison Brigham, DeVeaux School, Niagara Falls
Secretary/Treasurer, Clemewell Lay, Emma Willard School, Troy

1959
President, Clemewell Lay, Emma Willard School, Troy
Vice President, Gerald N. LaGrange, Rye Country Day School, Rye
Secretary/Treasurer, Della Simpson, Columbia School of Rochester, Rochester

1960
President, Gerald N. LaGrange, Rye Country Day School, Rye
Vice President, John Hodgdon, Pebble Hill School, DeWitt
Secretary/Treasurer, Della Simpson, Columbia School of Rochester, Rochester

1961
President, Gerald N. LaGrange , Rye Country Day School, Rye
Vice President, John Hodgdon, Pebble Hill School, DeWitt
Secretary/Treasurer, Helen Burtt Mason, The Berkeley Institute, Brooklyn

1962
President, E. Barton Chapin, Jr., The Park School of Buffalo, Buffalo
Vice President, Frank R. Miller, Hackley School, Tarrytown
Secretary/Treasurer, Helen Burtt Mason, The Berkeley Institute, Brooklyn

1963
President, E. Barton Chapin, Jr., The Park School of Buffalo, Buffalo
Vice President, Frank R. Miller, Hackley School, Tarrytown
Secretary/Treasurer, Elizabeth Vandemoer, St. Agnes School, Albany

1964
President, Frank R. Miller, Hackley School, Tarrytown
Vice President, David A. Kennedy, DeVeaux School, Niagara Falls
Secretary/Treasurer, Catherine Woodbridge, The Nightingale-Bamford School,
    Manhattan

1965
President, Frank R. Miller, Hackley School, Tarrytown
Vice President, David A. Kennedy, DeVeaux School, Niagara Falls
Secretary/Treasurer, Catherine Woodbridge, The Nightingale-Bamford School,
    Manhattan

1966
President, David A. Kennedy, DeVeaux School, Niagara Falls
Vice President, Walter Clark, North Country School, Lake Placid
Secretary, Jean Trembley Rich, Albany Academy for Girls, Albany
Treasurer, Catherine Woodbridge, The Nightingale-Bamford School, Manhattan

1967
President, David A. Kennedy, DeVeaux School, Niagara Falls
Vice President, Walter Clark, North Country School, Lake Placid
Secretary, Jean Trembley Rich, Albany Academy for Girls, Albany
Treasurer, James B. Draper, Pebble Hill School, Dewitt

1968
President, Walter Clark, North Country School, Lake Placid
Vice President, Stephen R. Hinrichs, The Harley School, Rochester
Secretary, Jean Trembley Rich, Albany Academy for Girls, Albany
Treasurer, James B. Draper, Pebble Hill School, Dewitt

1969
President, Walter Clark, North Country School, Lake Placid
Vice President, Stephen R. Hinrichs, The Harley School, Rochester
Secretary, Charlotte W. Mundy, The Professional Children's School, Manhattan
Treasurer, John Joline III, Darrow School, New Lebanon

1970
President, Stephen R. Hinrichs, The Harley School, Rochester
Vice President, Carl W. Andrews, Jr., Collegiate School, New York
Secretary, Charlotte W. Mundy, The Professional Children's School, Manhattan
Treasurer, John Joline III, Darrow School, New Lebanon

1971
President, Stephen R. Hinrichs, The Harley School, Rochester
Vice President, Gerald N. LaGrange, Rye Country Day School, Rye
Secretary, Charlotte W. Mundy, The Professional Children's School, Manhattan
Treasurer, John Joline III, Darrow School, New Lebanon

1972
President Gerald N. LaGrange, Rye Country Day School, Rye
Vice President, John F. Skillman, The Packer Collegiate Institute, Brooklyn
Secretary, Charlotte W. Mundy, The Professional Children's School, Manhattan
Treasurer, John Joline III, Darrow School, New Lebanon

1973

President, John F. Skillman, The Packer Collegiate Institute, Brooklyn
Vice President, Richard F. Barter, Collegiate School, Manhattan
Secretary, David Hume, St. David's School, Manhattan
Treasurer, John Joline III, Darrow School, New Lebanon

1974

President, John F. Skillman, The Packer Collegiate Institute, Brooklyn
Vice President, Richard F. Barter, Collegiate School, Manhattan
Secretary, David Hume, St. David's School, Manhattan
Treasurer, John Joline III, Darrow School, New Lebanon

1975

President, Richard F. Barter, Collegiate School, Manhattan
Vice President, Stephen Hinrichs, The Harley School, Rochester
Secretary, David Hume, St. David's School, Manhattan
Treasurer, John Joline III, Darrow School, New Lebanon

1976

President, Richard F. Barter, Collegiate School, Manhattan
Vice President, David Hume, St. David's School, Manhattan
Secretary, Mildred J. Berendsen, The Chapin School, Manhattan
Treasurer, John F. Skillman, Jr., The Packer Collegiate Institute, Brooklyn

1977

President, David Hume, St. David's School, Manhattan
Vice President, Christopher Wadsworth, The Nichols School, Buffalo
Secretary, Mildred J. Berendsen, The Chapin School, Manhattan
Treasurer, John F. Skillman, Jr., The Packer Collegiate Institute, Brooklyn

1978

President, David Hume, St. David's School, Manhattan
Vice President, Christopher Wadsworth, The Nichols School, Buffalo
Secretary, Joan McMenamin, The Nightingale-Bamford School, Manhattan
Treasurer, John F. Skillman, Jr., The Packer Collegiate Institute, Brooklyn

1979
President, Phillips Smith, Trinity Pawling School, Pawling
Vice President, Mildred J. Berendsen, The Chapin School, Manhattan
Secretary, Joan McMenamin, The Nightingale-Bamford School, Manhattan
Treasurer, John F. Skillman, Jr., The Packer Collegiate Institute, Brooklyn

1980
President, Phillips Smith, Trinity Pawling School, Pawling
Vice President, Mildred J. Berendsen, The Chapin School, Manhattan
Secretary, Frederic Withington, Friends Academy, Locust Valley
Treasurer, John F. Skillman, Jr., The Packer Collegiate Institute, Brooklyn

1981
President, Phillips Smith, Trinity Pawling School, Pawling
Vice President, Mildred J. Berendsen, The Chapin School, Manhattan
Secretary, David Hume, St. David's School, Manhattan
Treasurer, John F. Skillman, Jr., The Packer Collegiate Institute, Brooklyn

1982
President, Mildred J. Berendsen, The Chapin School, Manhattan
Vice President, Frederic Withington, Friends Academy, Locust Valley
Secretary, David Hume, St. David's School, Manhattan
Treasurer, Phillips Smith, Trinity Pawling School, Pawling

1983
President, Mildred J. Berendsen, The Chapin School, Manhattan
Vice President, Frederic Withington, Friends Academy, Locust Valley
Secretary, David Hume, St. David's School, Manhattan
Treasurer, Phillips Smith, Trinity Pawling School, Pawling

1984
President, Frederic Withington, Friends Academy, Locust Valley
Vice President, Joan McMenamin, The Nightingale-Bamford School, Manhattan
Secretary, John F. Skillman, Jr., The Packer Collegiate Institute, Brooklyn
Treasurer, Phillips Smith, Trinity Pawling School, Pawling

1985

President, Frederic Withington, Friends Academy, Locust Valley
Vice President, Joan McMenamin, The Nightingale-Bamford School, Manhattan
Secretary, Gardner P. Dunnan, The Dalton School, Manhattan
Treasurer, Phillips Smith, Trinity Pawling School, Pawling

1986

President, Joan McMenamin, The Nightingale-Bamford School, Manhattan
Vice President, Donald Abbott, Millbrook School, Millbrook
Secretary, Gardner P. Dunnan, The Dalton School, Manhattan
Treasurer, Phillips Smith, Trinity Pawling School, Pawling

1987

President, Joan McMenamin, The Nightingale-Bamford School, Manhattan
Vice President, Donald Abbott, Millbrook School, Millbrook
Secretary, Gardner P. Dunnan, The Dalton School, Manhattan
Treasurer, Phillips Smith, Trinity Pawling School, Pawling

1988

President, Donald Abbott, Millbrook School, Millbrook
Vice President, Joyce G. McCray, Friends Seminary, Manhattan
Secretary, Gardner P. Dunnan, The Dalton School, Manhattan
Treasurer, Phillips Smith, Trinity Pawling School, Pawling

1989

President, Donald Abbott, Millbrook School, Millbrook
Vice President, Gardner P. Dunnan, The Dalton School, Manhattan
Secretary, Neen Hunt, The Calhoun School, Manhattan
Treasurer, Phillips Smith, Trinity Pawling School, Pawling

1990

President, Gardner P. Dunnan, The Dalton School, Manhattan
Vice President, Peter Cobb, Nichols School, Buffalo
Secretary, Neen Hunt, The Calhoun School, Manhattan
Treasurer, Phillips Smith, Trinity Pawling School, Pawling

1991
President, Gardner P. Dunnan, The Dalton School, Manhattan
Vice President, Peter Cobb, Nichols School, Buffalo
Secretary, Andrew McLaren, Little Red School House & Elisabeth Irwin High
    School, Manhattan
Treasurer, Neen Hunt, The Calhoun School, Manhattan

1992
President, Peter Cobb, Nichols School, Buffalo
Vice President, Edes P. Gilbert, The Spence School, Manhattan
Secretary, Andrew McLaren, Little Red School House & Elisabeth Irwin High
    School, Manhattan
Treasurer, Gardner P. Dunnan, The Dalton School, Manhattan

1993
President, Peter Cobb, Nichols School, Buffalo
Vice President, Edes P. Gilbert, The Spence School, Manhattan
Secretary, Andrew McLaren, Little Red School House & Elisabeth Irwin High
    School, Manhattan
Treasurer, Roger B. Boocock, Riverdale Country School, Bronx

1994
President, Edes P. Gilbert, The Spence School, Manhattan
Vice President, Brian R. Walsh, The Buckley School, Manhattan
Secretary, Andrew McLaren, Little Red School House & Elisabeth Irwin High
    School, Manhattan
Treasurer, Roger B. Boocock, Riverdale Country School, Bronx

1995
President, Edes P. Gilbert, The Spence School, Manhattan
Vice President, Brian R. Walsh, The Buckley School, Manhattan
Secretary, Andrew McLaren, Little Red School House & Elisabeth Irwin High
    School, Manhattan
Treasurer, Roger B. Boocock, Riverdale Country School, Bronx

1996
President, Brian R. Walsh, The Buckley School, Manhattan
Vice President, Jeanne E. Amster, Ethical Culture Fieldston School, Manhattan
Secretary, Andrew McLaren, Little Red School House & Elisabeth Irwin High
    School, Manhattan
Treasurer, Roger B. Boocock, Riverdale Country School, Bronx

1997
President, Brian R. Walsh, The Buckley School, Manhattan
Vice President/Secretary, Andrew McLaren, Little Red School House & Elisabeth
    Irwin High School, Manhattan
Treasurer, Archibald A. Smith III, Trinity Pawling School, Pawling

1998
President, Andrew McLaren, Little Red School House & Elisabeth Irwin High
    School, Manhattan
Vice President, Nancy Salisbury, Convent of the Sacred Heart, Manhattan
Secretary, Charles Hertrick, Allendale Columbia School, Rochester
Treasurer, Archibald A. Smith III, Trinity Pawling School, Pawling

1999
President, Andrew McLaren, Little Red School House & Elisabeth Irwin High
    School, Manhattan
Vice President, Nancy Salisbury, Convent of the Sacred Heart, Manhattan
Secretary, Charles Hertrick, Allendale Columbia School, Rochester
Treasurer, Archibald A. Smith III, Trinity Pawling School, Pawling

2000
President, Archibald A. Smith III, The Trinity Pawling School, Pawling
Vice President, Thomas J. Reid, Buckley Country Day School, Roslyn
Secretary, Charles Hertrick, Allendale Columbia School, Rochester
Treasurer, Dorothy A. Hutcheson, The Nightingale-Bamford School, Manhattan

2001
President, Archibald A. Smith III, The Trinity Pawling School, Pawling
Vice President, Thomas J. Reid, Buckley Country Day School, Roslyn

Secretary, Charles Hertrick, Allendale Columbia School, Rochester
Treasurer, Dorothy A. Hutcheson, The Nightingale-Bamford School, Manhattan

2002

President, Charles Hertrick, Allendale Columbia School, Rochester
Vice President, Dorothy A. Hutcheson, The Nightingale-Bamford School,
    Manhattan
Secretary, Carol Gose DeVine, The Caedmon School, Manhattan
Treasurer, Drew Casertano, Millbrook School, Millbrook

2003

President, Charles Hertrick, Allendale Columbia School, Rochester
Vice President, Dorothy A. Hutcheson, The Nightingale-Bamford School,
    Manhattan
Secretary, Carol Gose DeVine, The Caedmon School, Manhattan
Treasurer, Drew Casertano, Millbrook School, Millbrook

2004

President, Dorothy A. Hutcheson, The Nightingale-Bamford School, Manhattan
Vice President, Drew Casertano, Millbrook School, Millbrook
Secretary, Carol Gose DeVine, The Caedmon School, Manhattan
Treasurer, Richard C. Bryan, Jr., Nichols School, Buffalo

2005

President, Dorothy A. Hutcheson, The Nightingale-Bamford School, Manhattan
Vice President, Drew Casertano, Millbrook School, Millbrook
Secretary, Carol Gose DeVine, The Caedmon School, Manhattan
Treasurer, Richard C. Bryan, Jr., Nichols School, Buffalo

2006

President, Drew Casertano, Millbrook School, Millbrook
Vice President, Richard C. Bryan, Jr., Nichols School, Buffalo
Secretary, Carol Gose DeVine, The Caedmon School, Manhattan
Treasurer, Stephen M. Clement III, The Browning School, Manhattan

2007

President, Drew Casertano, Millbrook School, Millbrook
Vice President, Richard C. Bryan, Jr., Nichols School, Buffalo
Secretary, Carol Gose DeVine, The Caedmon School, Manhattan
Treasurer, Stephen M. Clement III, The Browning School, Manhattan

2008

President, Richard C. Bryan, Jr., Nichols School, Buffalo
Vice President, Stephen M. Clement III, The Browning School, Manhattan
Secretary, Trudy Hall, Emma Willard School, Troy
Treasurer, Stephen Watters, The Green Vale School, Old Brookville

2009

President, Stephen M. Clement III, The Browning School, Manhattan
Vice President, Stephen Watters, The Green Vale School, Old Brookville
Secretary, Trudy Hall, Emma Willard School, Troy
Treasurer, Stephen Watters, The Green Vale School, Old Brookville

2010

President, Stephen M. Clement III, The Browning School, Manhattan
Vice President, Stephen Watters, The Green Vale School, Old Brookville
Secretary, Trudy Hall, Emma Willard School, Troy
Treasurer, Stephen Watters, The Green Vale School, Old Brookville

2011

President, Stephen Watters, The Green Vale School, Old Brookville
Vice President, Trudy Hall, Emma Willard School, Troy
Secretary, Dane L. Peters, Brooklyn Heights Montessori School, Brooklyn
Treasurer, Scott Gaynor, Stephen Gaynor School, Manhattan

2012

President, Stephen Watters, The Green Vale School, Old Brookville
Vice President, Scott Gaynor, Stephen Gaynor School, Manhattan
Secretary, Dane L. Peters, Brooklyn Heights Montessori School, Brooklyn
Treasurer, Susan Kambrich, Woodland Hill Montessori School, North Greenbush

2013

President, Scott Gaynor, Stephen Gaynor School, Manhattan
Vice President, Jody Douglas, The Buffalo Seminary, Buffalo
Secretary, Anthony G. Featherston IV, The Town School, Manhattan
Treasurer, Susan Kambrich, Woodland Hill Montessori School, North Greenbush

EXECUTIVE DIRECTORS

TENURE	NAME
1968-76	Dr. Appleton Mason
1976-86	Stephen Hinrichs
1986-2007	Frederick Calder
2007-09	Elizabeth "Penney" Riegelman
2009–Present	Dr. Mark Lauria

STAFF MEMBERS

TENURE	NAME	POSITION
1982-84	Joan Reed	Associate in the NYSAIS Office
1984-Present	Barbara Swanson	Associate Dir. for Professional Dev.
1987-2012	Lois (Lewis) Bailey	Associate Director
1994-97	Cathy A. Hoey	Administrative Assistant
1989-90	Lynn Schriner	Secretary
1997	Kenneth H. Barton	Deputy Executive Director
1998-2005	Jeanne E. Ryan	Administrative Assistant
2004-06	Andrew McLaren	Associate Executive Director
2006-07	Annie M. Nark	Administrative Assistant
2008-10	Gale Butler-Kuhlkin	Administrative Coordinator
2010-Present	Diana Wahrlich	Admin. Coord. for Business Services
2010-Present	Maria Flores	Admin. Coord. for Communications and Operations
2011-Present	Andrew Cooke	Technology Coordinator
2011-Present	Judith Sheridan, Ph.D.	Assoc. Dir. for Evaluation and Accreditation
2012-Present	George Swain	Assoc. Dir. for Evaluation and Accreditation
2013-Present	Dane L. Peters	ELAS Administrator

APPENDIX B

MEMBER SCHOOL LIST

SCHOOL	CITY/TOWN	FULL MEMBER YEAR
Abraham Joshua Heschel School	New York	1991
The Albany Academies	Albany	Pre-1966
All Souls School	New York	2012
Allen-Stevenson School	New York	1962
Allendale Columbia School	Rochester	1963 (merged 1971)
Anglo-American International School	New York	1980
Aurora Waldorf School	West Falls	2013
Bank Street School for Children	New York	1986
Barrow Street Nursery School at Greenwich House	New York	2011
Bay Ridge Preparatory School	Brooklyn	2008
The Berkeley Carroll School	Brooklyn	(Berkeley 1947; Carroll 1978; merged 1982)
The Birch Wathen Lenox School	New York	(Birch Wathen 1967; Lenox Pre-1966; merged 1991)
Buffalo Independent Secondary Schools Network (BISSNET)	Buffalo	
Blue School	New York	2013
The Brearley School	New York	1967
The Brick Church School	New York	1986
The British International School of New York	New York	
Brooklyn Friends School	Brooklyn	1975
Brooklyn Heights Montessori School	Brooklyn	1998
The Brookwood School	Cooperstown	1997, 2002
Brown School	Schenectady	1996
The Browning School	New York	Pre-1966

The Brownstone School	New York	2012
Buckley Country Day School	Roslyn	1966
The Buckley School	New York	1948
Buffalo Seminary	Buffalo	Pre-1966
The Caedmon School	New York	1972
The Calhoun School	New York	Pre-1966
Canisius High School	Buffalo	2000
The Cathedral School	New York	1976
Chaminade High School	Mineola	1987
The Chapin School	New York	Pre-1966
Chelsea Day School	New York	
The Children's Storefront	New York	1982
The Churchill School and Center	New York	1974
City and Country School	New York	1988
Collegiate School	New York	Pre-1966
Columbia Grammar and Preparatory School	New York	Pre-1966
Convent of the Sacred Heart	New York	1972
Cooke Center School	New York	2008
Corlears School	New York	1996
Cornelia Connelly Center	New York	2013
Cristo Rey New York High School	New York	2007
The Dalton School	New York	Pre-1966
Darrow School	New Lebanon	Pre-1966
De La Salle Academy	New York	1992
The Doane Stuart School	Rensselaer	1979
Dutchess Day School	Millbrook	1973
Dwight School	New York	1997
Early Steps	New York	2005
East Woods School	Oyster Bay	Pre-1966
Elmwood Franklin School	Buffalo	Pre-1966
Emma Willard School	Troy	Pre-1966
The Episcopal School	New York	1982
Ethical Culture Fieldston School	New York	1966
Fordham Preparatory School	Bronx	1987
French-American School of New York	Mamaroneck	1992

Friends Academy	Locust Valley	Pre-1966
Friends Seminary	New York	1978
Garden School	Jackson Heights	Pre-1966
The Gateway Schools	New York	1991
George Jackson Academy	New York	2004
German International School New York	White Plains	1984
The Gillen Brewer School	New York	2007
The Gow School	South Wales	Pre-1966
Grace Church School	New York	1970
Grace Episcopal Day School	Massapequa	1981
Green Meadow Waldorf School	Chestnut Ridge	1982
The Green Vale School	Old Brookville	Pre-1966
Hackley School	Tarrytown	Pre-1966
Hannah Senesh Community Day School	Brooklyn	2004
Harbor Country Day School	St. James	1962
Harlem Academy	New York	2010
The Harley School	Rochester	Pre-1966
The Harvey School	Katonah	Pre-1966
Hawthorne Valley Waldorf School	Ghent	1976
The Hewitt School	New York	Pre-1966
High Meadow School	Stone Ridge	2009
Hillel Community Day School	Rochester	2010
Holy Child Academy	Old Westbury	1971
Hoosac School	Hoosick	1968
Horace Mann School	Bronx	Pre-1966
The IDEAL School	New York	2006
Immaculata Academy	Hamburg	2004
The International Preschools	New York	2011
International School of Brooklyn	Brooklyn	2009
Keio Academy of New York	Purchase	1991
Kellenberg Memorial High School	Uniondale	1989
The Kew-Forest School	Forest Hills	Pre-1966
The Kildonan School	Amenia	1980
The Knox School	St. James	1979
La Scuola d'Italia Guglielmo Marconi	New York	1998
Lawrence Woodmere Academy	Woodmere	Pre-1966 (merged 1991)

LearningSpring School	New York	2006
Léman Manhattan Preparatory School	New York	2008
Little Red School House and Elisabeth Irwin High School	New York	1972
Long Island Lutheran	Brookville	2000
Long Island School for the Gifted	Huntington Station	2003
Loyola School	New York	1979
Lycée Français de New York	New York	1988
Madison Avenue Presbyterian Church Day School	New York	1992
Manhattan Country School	New York	1985
Manhattan High School for Girls	New York	1996
Manlius Pebble Hill School	DeWitt	Pre-1966
Maplebrook School	Amenia	1985
Martin Luther School	Maspeth	2001
Mary McDowell Friends School	Brooklyn	1994
Marymount School	New York	1970
The Masters School	Dobbs Ferry	1966
McQuaid Jesuit	Rochester	2012
Metropolitan Montessori School	New York	1993
Millbrook School	Millbrook	1966
Mizzentop Day School	Pawling	2003
New York Interschool	New York	2007
New York Military Academy	Cornwall-on-Hudson	1982
Nichols School	Buffalo	Pre-1966
The Nightingale-Bamford School	New York	Pre-1966
The Norman Howard School	Rochester	1980
North Country School	Lake Placid	Pre-1966
North Shore Hebrew Academy High School	Great Neck	2003
Northwood School	Lake Placid	Pre-1966
Notre Dame School of Manhattan	New York	
Oakwood Friends School	Poughkeepsie	Pre-1966
The Packer Collegiate Institute	Brooklyn	Pre-1966
The Park School of Buffalo	Snyder	Pre-1966
The Parkside School	New York	1999

Poly Prep Country Day School	Brooklyn	Pre-1966
Portledge School	Locust Valley	1967
Poughkeepsie Day School	Poughkeepsie	1979
Prep for Prep	New York	1991
Professional Children's School	New York	1963
Ramaz School	New York	1982
Regis High School	New York	1986
Resurrection Episcopal Day School	New York	2002
Rippowam Cisqua School	Bedford	1963
Riverdale Country School	Riverdale	Pre-1966
Robert C. Parker School	Wynantskill	2002
Robert College of Istanbul	New York	1982
Robert Louis Stevenson School	New York	1979
Rockland Country Day School	Congers	1963
Rodeph Sholom School	New York	1984
Ross School	East Hampton	2005
Rudolf Steiner School	New York	1987
Rye Country Day School	Rye	Pre-1966
Saint Ann's School	Brooklyn	1970
Saint David's School	New York	1967
Saint Francis Preparatory School	Fresh Meadows	1987
Saint Gregory's School	Loudonville	1967
SAR Academy & SAR High School	Riverdale	2009
Saratoga Independent School	Saratoga Springs	2006
Schechter School of Long Island	Jericho	2013
The School at Columbia University	New York	2005
School of the Holy Child	Rye	1983
The Smith School	New York	
Solomon Schechter School of Manhattan	New York	1997
Solomon Schechter School of Westchester	Hartsdale	2004
Soundview Preparatory School	Yorktown Heights	1992
The Spence School	New York	Pre-1966
St. Bernard's School	New York	Pre-1966
St. Hilda's & St. Hugh's School	New York	Pre-1966

St. Luke's School	New York	1978
St. Peter's by-the-Sea Day School	Bay Shore	1990
St. Thomas Choir School	New York	1967
Staten Island Academy	Staten Island	Pre-1966
Stephen Gaynor School	New York	1998
The Stony Brook School	Stony Brook	Pre-1966
Storm King School	Cornwall-on-Hudson	Pre-1966
The Studio School	New York	2005
Susan Odell Taylor School for Children	Troy	2007
The Town School	New York	1966
Trevor Day School	New York	1971
Trinity School	New York	1966
Trinity-Pawling School	Pawling	Pre-1966
Tuxedo Park School	Tuxedo Park	Pre-1966
Twin Parks Montessori Schools	New York	2006
United Nations International School	New York	1998
The Ursuline School	New Rochelle	1999
Village Community School	New York	1984
Vincent Smith School	Port Washington	1985
The Waldorf School of Garden City	Garden City	1975
The Waldorf School of Saratoga Springs	Saratoga Springs	2010
The Washington Market School	New York	2011
West End Day School	New York	1998
West Side Montessori School	New York	1993
Westbury Friends School	Westbury	1987
The Windsor School	Flushing	1996
The Windward School	White Plains	1986
The Winston Preparatory School	New York	1985
Woodland Hill Montessori School	North Greenbush	2004
Woodstock Day School	Woodstock	1999
Xavier High School	New York	1989
York Preparatory School	New York	1996

APPENDIX C

NYSAIS OFFICE LOCATIONS

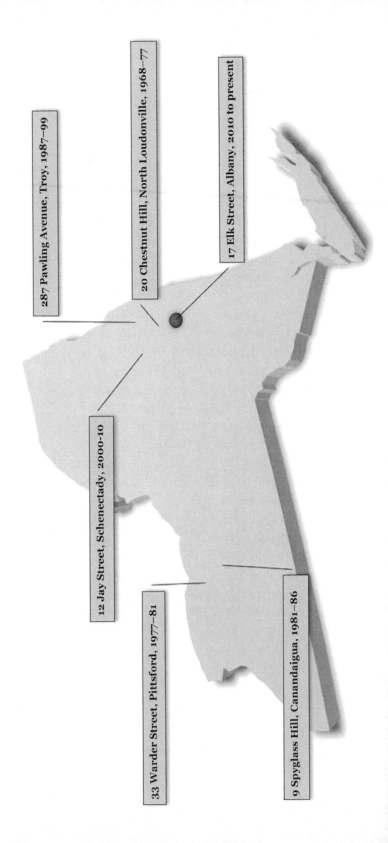

287 Pawling Avenue, Troy, 1987–99

20 Chestnut Hill, North Loudonville, 1968–77

17 Elk Street, Albany, 2010 to present

12 Jay Street, Schenectady, 2000–10

33 Warder Street, Pittsford, 1977–81

9 Spyglass Hill, Canandaigua, 1981–86

INDEX